ASSESSING LITERACY WITH THE LEARNING RECORD

Also available:
Assessing Literacy with the Learning Record
A Handbook for Teachers, Grades 6–12

ASSESSING LITERACY WITH THE LEARNING RECORD

A Handbook for Teachers, Grades K–6

Mary A. Barr, Dana A. Craig, Dolores Fisette,
and Margaret A. Syverson
Anne McKittrick, Editorial Assistant

HEINEMANN
Portsmouth, NH

Heinemann
A division of Reed Elsevier Inc.
361 Hanover Street
Portsmouth, NH 03801–3912
http://www.heinemann.com

Offices and agents throughout the world

The Learning Record Assessment System™ is administered by the Center for Language in Learning, under the direction of Dr. Mary A. Barr. The Center coordinates the work of a core group of U.S. teachers and administrators in maintaining and monitoring the system in registered schools, K–12.

The Learning Record and the Online Learning Record, under the direction of Dr. Margaret Syverson at the University of Texas, Austin (www.cwrl.utexas.edu/~syverson/olr), are adapted, with permission, from the work of the authors of the *Primary Language Record Handbook for Teachers*—Dr. Myra Barrs, Sue Ellis, Hilary Hester, and Anne Thomas—of the Centre for Language in Primary Education (CLPE), Webber Row Teacher's Centre, Webber Row, London SE1 8QW, England. The CLPE, directed by Myra Barrs, holds the copyright for Reading and Writing Scales 1 and 2 and the *PLR Handbook*, distributed in the U.S. by Heinemann. ISBN 0-435-08516-6. Reading and Writing Scales for high school are copyrighted and the system for large scale assessment using the Learning Record is trademarked by the Center for Language in Learning.

Both Centers collaborate in the ongoing development of this assessment model. For more information, contact the Center for Language in Learning, 10610 Quail Canyon Rd., El Cajon, CA 92021 (619) 443-6320. lrecord@cll.org, www.learningrecord.org/lrorg

The mission of the Center, a nonprofit organization with 501(c)(3) tax-exempt status, is to offer school districts and the concerned public a fair and accurate student evaluation system that integrates classroom-based assessment with teaching and learning. This handbook is part of the Learning Record Assessment System.™

Library of Congress Cataloging-in-Publication Data
Barr, Mary A. (Mary Anderson)
    Assessing literacy with the Learning Record : a handbook for teachers,
grades K–6 / Mary A. Barr . . . [et al.] ; editorial assistant, Anne McKittrick.
      p.   cm.
    Rev. ed. of: The Learning Record, c1998.
    Includes bibliographical references.
    ISBN 0-325-00117-0
    1. Portfolios in education—California—Handbooks, manuals, etc.
2. Academic achievement—California—Evaluation—Handbooks,
manuals, etc.   3. Education, Elementary—California—Evaluation—
Handbooks, manuals, etc.   4. Literacy—California—Handbooks, manuals,
etc. I. McKittrick, Anne.   II. Barr, Mary A. (Mary Anderson). Learning
Record. III. Title.
LB1029.P67B37   1999b
372.126'4'09794—dc21
                                                   98–45344
                                                   CIP

Editor: Lois Bridges
Production: Elizabeth Valway
Cover design: Darci Mehall, Aureo Design
Manufacturing: Louise Richardson

Printed in the United States of America on acid-free paper
03 02 01 00 99 ML 1 2 3 4 5

Contents

Foreword

The *Learning Record* (LR), as this handbook makes clear, is the product of an unusual piece of international collaboration between London and California. The British *Primary Language Record* (PLR) was developed in the late 1980s. It was a grassroots development involving teachers and schools across the whole of the inner-London area. Soon after the publication of its handbook in 1988 it became apparent that the PLR was interesting teachers in education systems far removed from London. The PLR offered these teachers an alternative framework for evaluation, one that made teachers' observations of students at work in the classroom central to any official record of their achievement.

Learning Record Introduced K–12

The reason why the *Primary Language Record* was so recognizable to an American audience was no doubt partly due to the fact that its view of literacy was strongly influenced by much important work on literacy published in the United States, as well as by the work of researchers in Australia and New Zealand. Its novelty, however, was that it offered a framework within which pupils' progress and development across the entire curriculum could be carefully tracked and recorded. The format and the guidance it provided enabled teachers to reflect on the relationship between students' reading and their writing, their oral language and their literacy development in first and second languages. It brought things together in a manageable frame.

It was the potential that the PLR offered for organizing work in the language arts that Mary Barr, then of the California Literature

Project and now director of the Center for Language in Learning, was quick to appreciate. Through her, the teachers at the Centre for Language in Primary Education in London entered into a long and productive partnership with teachers in California, which resulted in the development of the *California Learning Record*. The LR is now in use in many classrooms across California, and as this book makes clear, it is now, as in Britain, being extended to record students' learning beyond the Language Arts and the elementary classroom. Now known throughout the United States as the Learning Record Assessment System™, the comprehensive assessment described in this edition of the *Learning Record Handbook for Teachers, Grades K–6* ensures the trustworthiness of classroom assessment without a loss of favorable context for teaching and learning.

Everywhere today—and, most certainly, in England and the United States—the limitations of traditional testing arrangements are becoming clearer, and yet more is coming to depend on these inadequate measures. The search for ways of making students' actual achievements in the classroom count for evaluation purposes has obviously been a major factor powering the development and dissemination of the LR in California and now across the United States. The strength of the PLR and LR is that they provide a structure of portfolio assessment across the subject areas and enable teachers to be more fully accountable to parents and the public. There is impressive evidence in this book of how much more can be learned about students' progress from narrative records as well as strong positive feedback from parents or caregivers—who both contribute to the LR and are its first audience—about their preference for this kind of detailed information.

Making Classroom Learning Count

In today's diverse classrooms, there is a particular need for records that recognize difference and take note of the full range of students' linguistic and cultural experiences. Too often in the immediate educational past, differences between peoples were regarded as synonymous with deficit. By explicitly building on prior learning, the LR makes this learning from within and outside of school count in a school context, and may also indicate where each school needs to make changes in order to provide adequately for its community and for postsecondary needs.

This publication both introduces the Learning Record as a system of assessment that values and validates teacher judgment of academic progress and deepens our appreciation of what the PLR and LR can do. It helpfully documents the responses of both teachers and parents and/or caregivers to the student's record. It begins to answer fundamental questions about the kind of classroom management and curriculum design that facilitates observation. Through case studies, it shows us what happens in the staff development process as teachers take on this new and (initially) demanding way of working.

Above all, through the vivid pictures in the sample records themselves, it demonstrates the strength of evaluation based on narrative record keeping, and shows what happens when students learn to assess their own progress within a framework that is supportive and also flexible enough to accommodate difference. By charting the route that each individual takes toward full literacy, such records enable us as never before to map the diversity and complexity that previous records, based on a less comprehensive view of development, have tended to obscure.

Myra Barrs, Director
Centre for Language in
Primary Education, London

CLPE Director Myra Barrs (l) and Olivia O'Sullivan (r).

Anne Thomas (l) and Sue Ellis (r), members of the CLPE staff.

Using Assessing Literacy with the Learning Record

This handbook is written for teachers who are beginning to use the Learning Record in their own classes and for those who comprise a support staff for such teachers. Teacher educators will also find it useful with preservice teachers as they help teachers teach toward set standards.

The major part of the *Learning Record* handbook is organized around the four major sections of the LR: Part A, Data Collection, Part B, and Part C. Each of these sections includes rationale, processes, and examples with commentary from student records at Grades K–6. The examples have been collected over a period of ten years, during which the LR was piloted in hundreds of classrooms, and have been rewritten, typed, or edited for the sake of readability. All of the names of teachers, schools, and students have been masked.

■ Part A, which is usually completed during the first quarter of the year, features personal data about each student, including language background, physical challenges, the parents' or caregivers' description of the student as a learner, and the student's own description of his or her accomplishments and goals.

■ Throughout the year, teachers and students use operational content standards and performance criteria congruent with those set by the district and state to collect evidence about what and how the student is learning. Observation notes and samples of student work accumulate on the Data Collection Form, which is part of the LR.

■ Part B, completed near the end of the third quarter, calls for teacher summaries of the student's achievements accumulated in the Data Collection Form. Teachers use the descriptions in the Reading and Writing Scales, found in Appendix A, as criteria against which to assess the nature and extent of progress.

∎ Part C, completed at the end of the year, reviews and updates the student's achievements and provides suggestions for the student's continuing development.

Following these sections is a chapter on the kinds of classroom management and organization K–6 teachers have found useful. The handbook concludes with a description of the sustained and focused staff development required for successful implementation of the LR, in the classroom as well as across classrooms and schools.

These last two chapters are necessary for understanding how the *Learning Record* relates to ongoing efforts to improve learning for *all* students. They also make clear that this revamping of a classroom assessment program involves rethinking the role of teachers in assessment, the purpose of grades and test scores, and the support teachers can provide so their students can prepare themselves for a more complex future than today's adults have ever known.

In order to become familiar with how the LR fits into the school's calendar, readers may note on the time line provided in the Introduction how the various components of the LR can be organized and completed throughout the year.

Further information:
Center for Language in Learning
10610 Quail Canyon Rd.
El Cajon, CA 92021
Telephone (619) 443-6320

The LR is being used in schools across the United States in response to the need for measuring student achievement of school and state standards as well as the effects of school reform efforts. The Center for Language in Learning supports the efforts by

1. coordinating the services of a core group of LR teacher/coaches who lead professional development seminars in schools and districts as teachers phase in and maintain the use of this kind of assessment
2. producing materials (e.g., this handbook and computerized LR forms)
3. monitoring the quality assurance aspects of the assessment system to ensure that LR results across classrooms and districts are trustworthy from one year to the next
4. producing annual reports of student performance in reading and writing (by summer 1999, in mathematics, too)

Introduction

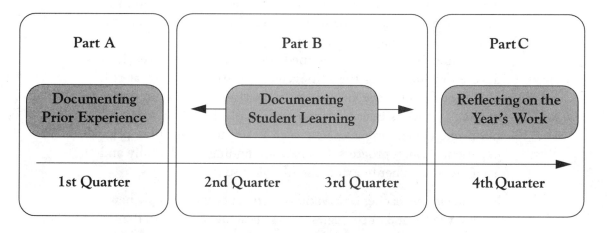

Introducing the Learning Record

The Learning Record (LR) yields a portfolio of information about a student's annual academic progress in K–12 classrooms. (This handbook provides information about the LR for teachers of Grades K–6; another has been developed for middle and high school teachers, Grades 6–12.) Judgments about the nature and extent of progress are based on evidence that students are meeting set standards as they engage in authentic language and literacy tasks, on information gained in consultations with parents or caregivers and the students themselves, and on analyses of student work.

Used in U.S. classrooms since 1988, the LR is an adaptation of the *Primary Language Record,* developed at the Centre for Language in Primary Education for K–6 use in London, England. In the United States, the model has expanded to include (1) the extension of the record of achievement to middle and secondary schools, using the base of literacy development to support students' academic progress in all subject areas; and (2) the development of a K–12 system of student assessment that validates teacher judgment of classroom work samples and observations for public accountability purposes.

Rationale for the Shift to the LR

The principles on which the LR rests are those designed to prepare students for the complexities of the information age, with emphases on:

❚ thoughtfulness over rote learning
❚ performance over assumptions of deficit
❚ individual development meshed with grade-level expectations and
❚ the strengths of being bilingual and of understanding cultures beyond one's own

In classrooms where these principles guide students, classroom assessment of student achievement occurs over time. Teachers recognize that assessment must be appropriate to the individual and to the subject matter under study, so students meet standards via different routes. For these reasons, many elementary teachers turn to the use of portfolios of student work from which they and their students can select samples for assessment purposes.

Although the LR is designed for all classrooms, teachers devoted to improving the achievement of students most at risk of school failure have taken the lead in its use. The academic progress of these students is sometimes masked by their scores on norm-referenced tests because such tests discount their prior experience. Such progress, teachers are finding, can be fully and accurately documented with the LR because it:

❚ encourages teacher observations of students as they apply new knowledge and/or strategies to tasks that are relevant to their prior experience
❚ shows the value of the prior knowledge students bring to school by relating it to school learning and
❚ helps teachers help students with what they need to learn, in the ways they learn best

The LR supports teachers as they move to portfolio assessment to help students become confident and reflective learners. It allows teachers, students, and their parents or other adult caregivers to assess learning throughout the year and from one year to the next without single-answer tests. Students demonstrate what they know in their oral discussions and presentations as well as in their reading and writing.

Teachers' observations of the learning in school, parents' observations of the learning at home, and students' self-assessments are

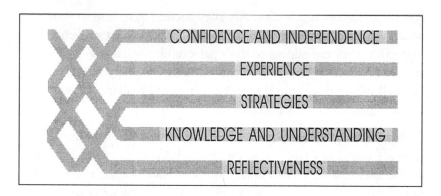

The Learning Record's five dimensions

documented throughout the year and corroborated in student work samples. Both the documentation and the corroborative samples are collected in a portfolio. Teachers summarize these observations of student accomplishment in terms of student progress toward local and statewide standards of achievement.

Centrality of Five Dimensions of Learning* in the LR

Integral to the LR are five dimensions of learning, which serve as a framework through which to view student learning. Teachers and their students evaluate student progress along continua of these five dimensions as students reveal what and how they are learning in oral classroom tasks as well as through their reading and their writing:

Confidence and independence. Are they willing to risk error? Are they increasingly able to volunteer information and possible solutions to problems, to ask questions, and to initiate topics for discussion and study? Are they willing to persevere in the face of complexity?

Experience. Are they using their prior knowledge to make sense of their current tasks and projects? Is there evidence to show that they have broadened and deepened their experience in specific curricular areas? Can they apply their school experience to a range of authentic purposes?

Strategies. Are they using the skills and strategies of the subject to solve problems and construct projects and products? Do they demonstrate they can read, write, listen, and speak with increasing effectiveness across a range of genre and audience appropriate to particular disciplines and areas of interest?

---

* The five dimensions of learning have been adapted for use in the LR from the work of the Centre of Language in Primary Education, authors of the *Primary Language Record.* Their publication in 1990 of *Patterns of Learning* featured these dimensions in terms of language development. The California teachers who developed the LR found them useful also in describing the development of learning generally.

Knowledge and understanding. Are they increasingly able to show what they have come to know and understand? What evidence is there that they are adding to their personal knowledge and understanding? What evidence does their language (their reading, writing, talking, and listening) reveal about their broader and deeper knowledge in a given subject?

Reflectiveness. Are they increasingly able to describe how and what they are learning to do and to understand? Can they provide criteria for assessing their own work? Are they developing the ability to judge the quality of their own work? Do they know what to do to improve it?

How the LR Works

The focus of the LR is on students in the process of learning as well as on the work they complete as a result of course tasks. Both teachers and students can set these tasks as well as the criteria for the quality of the work students produce. As students mature, they take on more and more aspects of assessing their work.

Teachers collect information about learning from students and their parents or mentors early in the school year, documenting student literacy and subject matter experience, interests, past successes, and future goals. With this knowledge as a base, student portfolios store such data as notes, papers, logs, lists, quotations, drawings, and observations regarding student performance in a range of settings, from one-on-one conferences to participation in large-group and peer-group activities.

Throughout the year, teachers help students collect observations, notes, and student work samples, which they collaboratively summarize in three sections. In Part A of the LR, completed during the first quarter of the school year, teachers record details of two activities—a discussion between teacher and parent or mentor about the student's learning history and a discussion between teacher and student about his or her prior literacy and subject matter experience. When appropriate, teachers conduct the discussion in the parents' native language with the help of community aides or other family members.

For Part B, completed over the second and third quarters, teachers, and their students as they mature, collect observation notes and summarize them to reveal what students have shown they know and know how to do in regard to course objectives. Teachers also help students reflect on the kinds of experiences that have helped each of them learn best. As students take on much more of the data collection and record keeping, they learn to apply sets of criteria to their own work samples and to monitor their own progress toward meeting performance standards.

Part C summarizes and updates accomplishments during the final quarter. In this section, parents, teachers, and students review the year's record, and the teacher comments on what comes next.

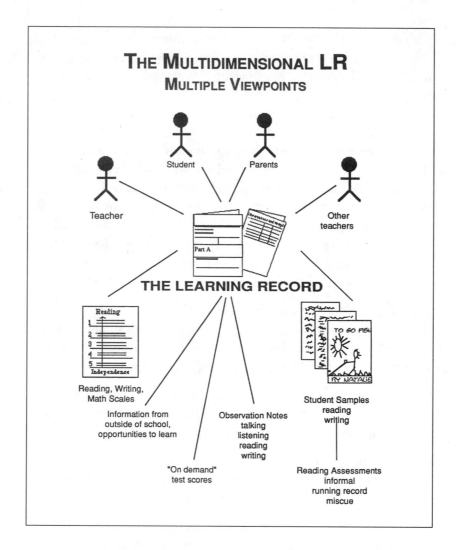

The Multidimensional Learning Record

No Set Learning Tasks or Required Readings

The LR assessment system does not require prescribed tasks because there is no one way to approach teaching and learning anything. The LR format, however, is standardized to permit parents and other teachers at the school and/or at other schools to review student records easily. Because people are multifaceted in their interests and attributes, the format permits multiple sources of evidence about student learning and literacy:

❚ parent descriptions of home literacy (Parts A and C)
❚ student work samples and reflections (Parts A, B, and C)
❚ teacher and student observations and analyses of the work samples (Part B Data Collection)
❚ teacher summaries of what the data means in terms of student achievement (Part B)
❚ teacher recommendations about what's next to be learned (Parts B and C)

Teachers and their students collect this evidence of student learning, including placement on the appropriate reading performance scale, in Parts A and B. (Part C is an update of the summaries in Part B.)

In order to help teachers assess student performance according to acknowledged standards without standardizing performance, the LR allows students to show what they can do in their own unique ways. On the basis of the observations and the work samples, a fifth-grade teacher will describe a student's achievement in reading, for example, on a continuum ranging from that of "a less experienced reader" to "an exceptionally experienced reader." The terms, when illustrated by actual evidence of student work that fits the description to which these and intermediate labels are fixed, communicate the present level of reading and what must be achieved to reach the next higher level.

The LR and Restructuring Schools

While the LR may seem "merely" a way to assess student performance, the following characteristics combine to support schoolwide restructuring of curriculum, instruction, *and* assessment:

❚ As a portfolio assessment method for all K–12 students, the LR is especially useful because it acknowledges and builds on the prior experience of each learner, including the learner with special needs.

❚ Based on current theory, research, and good practice about how students develop literacy in each subject area, it encourages extensive experience with a range and variety of texts.

❚ It helps learners focus on the construction of meanings in increasingly complex texts by using a range of skills and strategies.

❚ It recognizes the intertwined nature of reading, writing, talking, and listening.

❚ Its implementation model supports teachers as they gain expertise in assessing student achievement by reviewing the quality of student work.

❚ It involves students, their parents, and all teachers in observing progress in five important dimensions of learning, not only on what can be measured on a test.

❚ It documents the literacy development of both monolingual and bilingual students across a linguistic range.

❚ It links a classroom assessment system to a broader system of school and student assessment necessary for program evaluation and public accountability.

❚ It provides performance scales congruent with desired outcomes described in national and state standards.

But Is the LR a Trustworthy Assessment System?

Answers to the following questions, provided by Dr. Royce Sadler, professor of education at Griffith University in Brisbane, Queensland, Australia,[1] explain the trustworthy qualities of the LR:

What exactly is the Learning Record?

First, it is much more than a special type of report card, although the Learning Record is indeed part of a system of assessing and reporting student achievement. It achieves these ends in ways that recognize the different ways children learn, and the different ways in which their learning is expressed. When a school uses the Learning Record, it becomes part of a system that produces both detailed and summary information about how students in regular and special classes are performing.

What is the basic philosophy behind the Learning Record?

Teachers, by virtue of their close association with their students, develop an extensive knowledge of how their students are achieving. That knowledge is rich and highly contextualized: the teacher knows the history of a student's growth in achievement, sees many things the student does and produces, and progressively builds up a large body of information. This information forms the basis of judgments about how much the student has learned, and the form that learning has taken. The Record provides a systematic way of tapping into that information, and of analyzing and reporting it.

Won't teachers' judgments be colored by their knowledge of students as persons?

The Learning Record is part of a system that draws upon the cumulative experience of teachers who collaboratively agree to keep themselves professionally calibrated, so Records from one school or classroom are comparable with Records from other schools and classrooms.

Hasn't research shown that teacher judgments and grades are unreliable?

Some research does indeed show that teacher judgments about the quality of student work is unreliable. Unreliability means that the

---

1. Royce Sadler holds advanced degrees in mathematics and education. Originally a high school teacher, he has taught mathematics and computer programming at two institutes of technology, and courses in assessment and testing at two Australian universities. In 1985, he worked for the Queensland Board of Secondary School Studies as Head of its Assessment Unit, and helped to provide theoretical foundations for school-based assessment, with particular focus on defining and communicating achievement standards for purposes very similar to those used by the Learning Record. He has published widely on assessment issues, and has a particular interest in making assessment effective in promoting learning. Dr. Sadler's 1987 paper on the theoretical basis for "standards-referenced" assessment in the *Oxford Review of Education* informed the development of the Learning Record Assessment System™.

same teacher may grade student work differently on different occasions, or that different teachers may grade the same work differently. But by and large these studies have been carried out by simply asking teachers to regrade or cross-grade student work without the benefit of professionally designed systems that could lead to improvement. The Record aims to provide systematic and well-grounded support for teachers in making their judgments.

This all sounds very subjective. Surely we want objective assessments, particularly when students' futures are at stake!

It is true that teacher judgments are subjective. But that does not necessarily make them random or worthless. In fact, if teacher judgments were hopelessly woolly or unreliable, the profession of teaching might as well be abolished. In any case, most professional assessments (not just those in education), and most of the decisions we make in daily life, are subjective in the sense that they are made by people. This does not, in itself, make them dubious or hollow. Subjective judgments cover the full spectrum, from those that are mostly matters of taste or simple preference (such as liking strawberry ice cream), to those that are more serious in their consequences but are based on weak evidence or guesswork (or even wishful thinking), to those that are soundly based on clear evidence. To question judgments simply because they are subjective would lead to a rejection of most of the decisions made in everyday life. So the real issue is not whether judgments are subjective or objective, but how consistent those judgments are, how meaningfully they can be interpreted, and whether good consequences follow.

It seems to me that students need to be tested, so that they all complete the same tasks, the scores are worked out, and then the scores are compared with norms. Numbers are objective, and we know what they stand for.

All assessment of student achievement (whether the tests are teacher-made or nationwide) involves subjective judgments. Test items are constructed by people, pretested on people, and refined, rejected, or retained by people. The criteria on which these decisions are based are debated among experts, and decisions are made about which criteria to use and how to use them. Every worthwhile testing program is the result of deliberation, and alternative choices could always have been made. With standardized testing, all of the subjective judgment goes on behind the scenes, but it is there (and important) nevertheless. The final stages of testing programs involve administration of the test, scoring, and comparison of individual scores with state or national norms. These phases may perhaps seem to be more overtly objective or scientific. The scores have an "objective" meaning primarily in the sense that experts agree on what the correct answer is, and that the resulting scores are numbers that can be processed statistically. But the judgments that give rise to the numbers, as is indeed the prior decision to measure performance using these techniques, are subjective decisions. So the debate is not between subjectivity and objectivity as such, but how credible, how consistent, and how meaningful the assessments are.

Are you saying then that standardized testing is not concerned about being credible, consistent, and meaningful?

Not at all. Standardized testing is interested in these goals, but approaches the problem from one particular angle. It puts the subjectivity in at the front end; then the formal processing procedures take over. The Learning Record, on the other hand, tackles the "quality-of-assessment" problem from a quite different direction. It aims to exploit the rich, specific, and contextualized knowledge teachers develop about their students, and make that the basis for a system of recording and reporting achievement. The Learning Record keeps teacher professional judgments right in there until the end. But it continues to place a high premium on credibility, consistency, and meaningfulness, and of course on high-quality evidence for the judgments.

So apart from the techniques, the two are basically the same?

The Learning Record aims to establish a standards-based framework to enable student achievement to be assessed and reported. It is fundamentally different in that the standards are not numerical cutoffs from a testing program, but have an entirely different, but equally rigorous, formulation. The standards are related not to test scores, but directly to what students have done. The standards themselves are decided upon, field-tested, and refined with the help of assessment experts. They take the form of specific descriptions of behaviors and performance together with concrete examples (called *exemplars*) to make the meaning of the descriptions quite clear. A particular student's performance is observed (in context) and compared with the relevant set of standards. The teacher's function is to match the student's performance with the standards definition that fits best. The various standards are given numerical labels, and they constitute a scale to allow for communication between teachers and among teachers, students, and parents. The performances of students on the scales can be aggregated to provide system-wide performance summaries. So you see, the focus is primarily on how individual student performance can be identified directly and linked to a system of standards, using the teacher's judgments.

But these judgments could be based on different evidence for different students. Isn't that open to question?

The Learning Record is essentially about obtaining evidence about student performance before a judgment is made about the level of performance. The evidence can take a variety of forms, but conclusions are not reached on evidence that is irrelevant, skimpy, or of poor quality. The main differences between the Learning Record and standardized testing are that the Record draws on a much more extensive data base than a single testing episode, and that the evidence is generated mostly, but not necessarily exclusively, through normal classroom and learner activity. This not only increases the validity of the evidence, but also ensures that crucial decisions are not made on the basis of a single test event. In other words, the Learning Record is open to multiple sources of evidence, and these are weighed up together. It follows that different students may produce evidence in different ways, but all of it reflects the learning that has taken place.

Could the Learning Record be used alongside other forms of testing?

Indeed it could. And it will produce results that are soundly based in calibrated teacher judgments.

What exactly do you mean by "calibrated" judgments?

Teachers operating in their classrooms by themselves constantly make judgments about how their students are progressing. That is part of what it means to be a teacher. But when teachers participate in the Learning Record (as an assessment system), they agree to use prescribed procedures that provide a basis for comparable judgments to be made between different teachers, in different schools, and at different times. The aim is to ensure consistent interpretation and application of the standards. By keeping themselves knowledgeable about the standards that have been defined, and through using them in accordance with the set procedures to arrive at judgments that are consistent with the standards (and hence with the judgments other teachers would make, given the same evidence), teachers are said to be "calibrated."

Tell me again, how are these "standards" defined?

The main features are verbal descriptions of the qualities required of work at the different levels. This is complemented by concrete examples of work, to illustrate the descriptions. These two, the descriptors and the exemplars, are key elements of the learning scales for different fields of learning. The exemplars show, and the descriptions tell. They work together. But that is not all. Teachers working within the system participate in moderation meetings with other teachers, so that their own ability to make judgments is kept consistent with other teachers and with the standards as set out in the scales. A spin-off on the system is that students themselves have access to the scale points, and both teachers and parents have available a direct way of seeing exactly what the standards mean. Having access to the standards provides an open system that is both helpful to students and closely aligned with what goes on in class. In fact, the close correspondence between what is assessed and normal classroom activity is an important strength of the Learning Record system.

With "external" forms of testing, the students and the teacher are pitted against a common enemy, the test. The Learning Record places the teacher in the position of being both coach and judge. Won't this adversely affect the teaching relationship?

The design of the Learning Record is such that the standards do have an external formulation, and they are accessible to both the teacher and the learner. The student can actually see examples of what the standards imply, and can work with the teacher toward improving personal performance. If you like, both teacher and learner are "assessed" against the standards, and remain partners. It's not unlike athletic training, where goals (and expectations) are set and the aim is to attain them. But in athletics, of course, the goals can often be set down simply as times or distances. Educational outcomes are considerably more complicated, which is why the standards themselves can't be left to chance (or worse, not determined at all). They need careful thought, trial, and analysis. Just collecting evidence is not in itself enough. The evidence must be sifted, understood, and related to a scale of performance. And of course how other students perform at the time is of secondary interest.

How do teachers find the system? Don't they feel their reputation as professionals is undermined?

Quite the reverse. Most teachers using the system welcome the collaboration with other teachers, and want their judgments to be consistent with those of other competent professionals. They see this as part of their professional responsibility as a teacher, just as the public expects other professions to make sound, consistent judgments. Teachers using the Record are not wedded to the idea that their own (perhaps idiosyncratic) judgments are automatically infallible, even if they are very experienced. And, of course, the Learning Record still leaves teachers with a great deal of professional autonomy as to what goes on in their classrooms.

How do students react to this? Don't they expect the teacher to tell them how they are doing?

A central premise of the Learning Record is that students, as part of their learning, need to develop the ability to make reasoned judgments about the quality of their own work. This is for two reasons. The first is that students need to learn how to manage the quality of their own work while they are actually producing it. Otherwise they have to depend on the teacher to tell them how they are doing, and have limited opportunity to learn otherwise. Even young children are capable of making judgments, and part of the teacher's responsibility is to help them refine their judgments. Second, learners ultimately need to take responsibility for their own learning, and learning how to do this starts in school. It can only come about by giving learners true experience in making judgments, preferably about work of the same type they are attempting to produce themselves. The Learning Record provides a creative and supportive environment for this to occur. The evidence to date shows two things: students like to become involved in collaborative assessment with the teacher, and the doing of it makes a big, positive difference to learning itself and to learners' attitudes about learning.

Credits

Valuable models and collegial assistance to the ongoing development of the LR Assessment System™ have been generously given since 1988 by the staff members from the Centre for Language in Primary Education Webber Row Teachers Centre, Webber Row, London, SE1 8QW. Thanks to Myra Barrs, Sue Ellis, Hilary Hester, Olivia O'Sullivan, and Anne Thomas.

The educators named below are members of the California LR Core Development Group. They have contributed results of their ongoing classroom research to the overall design and implementation of the Learning Record Assessment System™. They are certified to serve as on-site coaches in the implementation of the system.

Name	School District
Bobbie Allen	UC San Diego
Leslie Barkley	Ukiah Unified
Diane Cook	Ferndale Unified
Win Cooper	UC San Diego
Gretchen Covington	Sebastopol Union
Dana A. Craig	Lakeside Union
Lisa Damico	Petaluma City Schools
Rena Ferrero	Woodland Joint Unified
Dolores Fisette	Willits Unified
Chris Funtas	Lakeside Union
Janet Ghio	Lincoln Unified
Phyllis Hallam	John Swett Unified & UC Berkeley, doctoral student
Carol Hendsch	Fresno Unified
Gloria Jarrell	Ukiah Unified
Kiyo Masuda	Fresno Unified
Judy McGrew	Lincoln Unified
Joel Monge	Pomona Unified
Gail Munnecke	LA Co. Office of Education
Muriel Olsen	Merced City Schools
Amauri Rodriguez	Pomona Unified
Katharine Sparrow	Ukiah Unified

Name	School District
Sally Thomas	*Claremont Graduate School*
Carol Updegraff	*Ukiah Unified*
Stefanie Watson	*Pacific Union*
Kellie Welty	*Woodland Joint Unified*

Critical Friends of the Center for Language in Learning

Name	Position
Annie Calkins	*Assistant Superintendent, Juneau Schools, Juneau, Alaska*
Patrick Dias	*Professor Emeritus, Teacher Education, McGill University, Montreal*
Sandra Fox	*School Reform Team Leader, Bureau of Indian Affairs, Department of the Interior, Washington, D.C.*
Angela Garcia-Sims	*Consultant, WestEd; former director of curriculum and assessment, South Bay School District, Imperial Beach, CA*
Saul Krimsly	*Independent technology consultant, Intelligent Solutions, Potter Valley, CA*
Monty Neill	*Executive Director, FairTest*
Jesse Perry	*President, International Federation of Teachers of English; Past President, National Council of Teachers of English; Retired, Language Arts Specialist, San Diego City Schools*
Royce Sadler	*Professor of education, Griffith University in Brisbane, Queensland, Australia and former Head of the Queensland Board of Secondary School Studies Assessment Unit*
Margaret Syverson	*Associate professor of rhetoric and composition and associate director of Computer and Research Laboratory, University of Texas, Austin*
Carmen Taylor	*Program Director, National Indian School Board Association*
John Willis	*Senior analyst, PRC Education and Evaluation Services in Indianapolis, Indiana, and field consultant, Region VII Comprehensive Center in Norman, Oklahoma*

Documenting Prior Experience

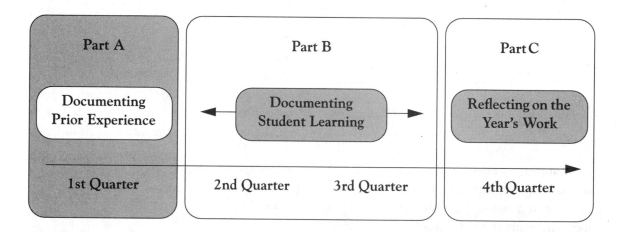

Teachers complete the front page of the Learning Record during the first quarter or term. It consists of a section containing general information about the student and Part A for recording the summaries of two discussions: a discussion between the parent and the teacher (A1) and a discussion between the student and the teacher (A2). In Part A, teachers record what parents or other caregivers say about the students as learners as well as what the students themselves have to say on the same topic. It is important to remember, in regard to gathering such information, that the LR is *not* a confidential document. Information written on the form, therefore, should reflect the understanding that the LR is an open record of accomplishment.

The teacher needs to know the student's date of birth so maturation can be taken into account, the student's language background, any physical challenges, and the names of other staff members who will also be contributing to the student's learning record.

Students in the class may speak more than one language. Some may be learning English. This section provides space for what languages are understood or spoken as well as what languages can be read and written so that a teacher can tap into all the student's linguistic strengths.

The Learning Record (Elementary)

Adapted with permission from the Primary Language Record (PLR). Developed and copyrighted by the Centre for Language in Primary Education, Webber Row Teacher's Centre, Webber Row, London SE1 8QW, in 1988 and distributed in the U.S. by Heinemann Educational Books, Inc. ISBN 0-435-08516-6

School   Teacher   School Year

Name   Grade Level _____   Birth Date _____
                              Boy/Girl _____

Languages understood	Languages read	Languages spoken	Languages written

Details of any aspect of hearing, vision, or coordination affecting the child's language/literacy. Give the source and date of this information.

Names of staff involved with child's development.

PART A To be completed during the first quarter

A1 Record of discussion between child's parent(s) and class teacher (LR Handbook for teachers K-6, Part A1)

Signed Parent(s) _____   Teacher _____
            Date _____

A2 Record of language/literacy conference with child (LR Handbook for teachers K-6, Part A2)

Date _____

Published as a component of The Learning Record Assessment System.™ For further information, call or write the Center for Language in Learning at 10610 Quail Canyon Road, El Cajon, CA 92021 (619) 443-6320.

FIGURE 1–1 Front page of the Learning Record (Elementary)

Language development in the student's home language can support language development in a second or third language. How long the student has been acquiring English or another language and information about oral capabilities or reading fluency in the home language, for example, will give a fuller picture of the student's experience and allow the teacher to plan instruction that builds on that experience.

A1 and A2: Parent and Student Conferences

The purpose of the A1 parent conference is to draw on the knowledge that parents have about the student. This discussion will allow parents to share knowledge of students at home that has relevance for their learning at school. Parents can contribute their observations of how their children learn best, what they know about their children's inter-

ests, and what their hopes and concerns are for their children's futures. The goals set at this conference can be reviewed and new ones set the following year.

The A2 student conference is intended to give students an opportunity to talk about themselves as learners. It will also show the teacher what students perceive as their strengths and weaknesses, and what goals and interests they have. As the LR is used by teachers throughout the school, students and their parents can begin to compare year-to-year achievements and to set criteria for measuring success in their own terms.

The value of this conference for students is that it helps them link their world outside the school with what they must do for success in school. Because the LR will show what and how the student learns throughout the year, students contribute the "baseline data" in A2 from which to measure accomplishment. Upper-grade students, especially, need to assess their own experience as readers, writers, and learners and to set the direction for the year's work in these areas. The pages that follow in this section are devoted to descriptions of how teachers use Parts A1 and A2 with accompanying examples.

A1 Parent Conference: Record of Discussion Between Parent (or Caregiver) and Teacher

Juan's parents tell his teacher: "He is very creative. He likes to draw. He enjoys puzzles and games. He is patient." These quotes not only provide insights into this second grader's learning habits and preferences; they also reveal the values they want reinforced in the classroom. Because of the valuable information to be gained, this parent-teacher discussion needs to occur during the first quarter of the year. School staffs, after piloting with a few parents, often find the information they receive is so valuable they incorporate the discussion into their conference schedule or add it. Typically, the discussion takes about fifteen minutes. The quality of the discussion will be enhanced if some questions are considered ahead of time:

■ How will the parent be contacted? By phone? Letter?

■ If the parent speaks a language other than English and the teacher does not, can an interpreter be present? This might be a friend of the family, an older sibling or relative, or another faculty member.

■ What provisions can be made for divorced parents?

■ Will one or two conferences be held?

■ Can the conference be recorded for summarizing later with parent permission for the summary?

It should be clear from the beginning of the conference that the student is the focus for the discussion. The parent should understand that the teacher needs this information. The teacher's role in the discussion is that of an information gatherer. Parents also benefit from the experience. As one second-grade teacher put it, "I've seen it help parents understand their child better as well as focus my thinking on student progress and next steps." A fifth-grade teacher reported that once parents learned from others about the nature of the conference, they began to hunt for her before, during, and after school, "fearing I would be missing something important if they didn't get to talk to me."

Who will write on the form? Do notes need to be taken during the conference? Maybe the conference can be summarized at the end of the discussion. Teachers will need to keep in mind that this is an open record of accomplishment. Items that are confidential should not be written on the record.

Teachers often remark that this type of conference is quite different from the traditional conferences they have conducted in the past. A teacher may feel a bit awkward starting the discussion. A good way to begin is

to explain the LR and to ask the parent's help in completing the sections at the top of the LR form. Or it might be as simple as saying to the parent, "Tell me whatever you think will help me support your child's learning—for example, his or her special interests, learning habits, opportunities, or accomplishments."

It may be necessary from time to time to refocus the conference on how the student learns best and on what the parent knows that can help the student in school, with questions such as these:

"What does the student enjoy reading and writing at home?"

"What have parents observed about the student's use of language(s) at home?"

"Are there opportunities at home for selecting books, writing on topics chosen by the student, discussing books and TV, or using computers?"

"What are the student's favorite TV programs?"

"What changes have parents observed in the student's language and literacy development?"

"What goals would parents like to set for this year?"

The parent or caregiver will need an opportunity to read and approve the summary of his/her contribution that becomes part of the Record.

Examples of the Initial Parent Conference
The records of discussions between parents and teachers help us realize the range of experiences that parents provide for students at home.

The conference between George's parent and his teacher, described in Figure 1–2, shows that George engages in many rich learning activities at home. His parent is obviously aware of his challenges in becoming a reader. It is interesting to note that the parent clearly provided information in each of the five dimensions of learning.

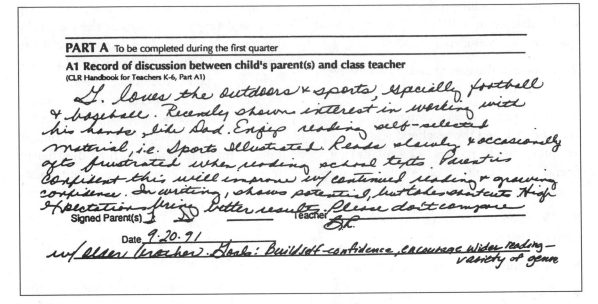

PART A To be completed during the first quarter

A1 Record of discussion between child's parent(s) and class teacher
(CLR Handbook for Teachers K–6, Part A1)

J. loves the outdoors & sports, specially football & baseball. Recently shown interest in working with his hands, like Dad. Enjoys reading self-selected material, i.e. Sports Illustrated. Reads slowly & occasionally gets frustrated when reading school texts. Parent is confident this will improve w/ continued reading & growing confidence. In writing, shows potential, but takes shortcuts. High Expectations bring better results. Please don't compare

Signed Parent(s) ___   Teacher ___

Date 9·20·91

w/ class teacher. Goals: Build self-confidence, encourage wider reading — variety of genre

FIGURE 1–2   Grade Five, boy. Language: English

PART A To be completed during the first quarter

A1 Record of discussion between student's parent(s) and class teacher (Discussion may have taken place in writing, by phone or in face-to-face conference)   (See CLR Handbook for Teachers, A1).

N has always enjoyed school and in particular language arts. She reads at any opportunity. Mom says that N enjoys reading and that both parents read to N as a child. There are many magazines and books at home, and mrs. often take both daughters to the library. N had the same teacher in 4th and 5th grade. She sparked N's interest in writing and since that time, N has written at home. She writes poems, short stories, mini books and journals. N is very theatrical and enjoys acting and performing.

Date 10/14/92

FIGURE 1–3   Grade Six, girl. Language: English

Nana's parents, (Figure 1–3), have provided her with many language and literacy experiences at home: being read to, going to the library, enacting, writing in a variety of genres. They are aware of how her previous teachers have helped promote her love of reading and are able to communicate the value they place on Nana's talents. They will be very pleased to learn that their daughter's teacher this year will continue to build on her successes thus far.

Yolanda's parents show, in Figure 1–5, they also provide their child with many literacy experiences at home. They reveal, in addition, that they want her to learn English without sacrificing her first language, Spanish. By having this conversation early in the year, Yolanda's teacher can collaborate with

> M. loves books. loves to be read to; brings home a "truckload" from the library
> M. has books in both languages he is learing to speak more Croatian as he is read to. He is comfortable speaking in Croatian when visiting Yugoslavia.
> Was able to read *Ferdinand* when he got it on the book order.
>
> Signed Parent(s) _____ ———— Teacher ___ *Judy L* ___
>
> Date ___ 11-6-90 ___

FIGURE 1–4   Grade One, boy. Languages: English, Croation

PART A To be completed during the first quarter

A1 Record of discussion between child's parent(s) and class teacher
(CLR Handbook for Teachers K-6, Part A1)

> Y. talks about school a lot at home.. She likes to play outside, she colors, she plays school with her little brother. She is the teacher. She has a chalkboard to draw and color. Y. will ask if she has trouble reading a word. Mom is going to start teaching Y. to read and write in Spanish. Y. talked to both her parents. "Y. wants to come to school even when she is sick."

Signed Parent(s) _____   Teacher_____

Date ___ 10-11 ___

FIGURE 1–5   Grade Two, girl. Languages: Spanish, English

her parents to support her learning in both languages. Mike's parents, too, suggest their eagerness to help their child maintain the language of the grandparents and parents, and they realize how important it is to have books in both languages.

Kenny C.'s parent conference (Figure 1–6) reveals that he brings to school much confidence and zeal as a language user. In addition to describing her child as one who pretends to read, an early literacy trait for most children, the parent also notes other

information the teacher can use to provide learning-to-read opportunities for Kenny C. in school. For one thing, the parent reveals that Kenny C. associates books with speaking English. Knowing this, his teacher can foster his emerging biliteracy, perhaps by having him "practice read" to his little sister, in English or in Mien. By connecting his oral strengths and his family practices to what he is learning about reading and writing in school, Kenny C. will have rich, sustained support at home.

A1 Record of discussion between child's parent(s) and class teacher

After K.C. finishes his homework, he plays with toys and draws. He talks as he works. Sometimes he takes care of his little sister. When he takes books, he seems to be reading it. He talks in English about the book. He does his own homework. When K.C. speaks with somebody, he doesn't talk too much; but when he's reading books he talks a lot. He doesn't open a book without talking.

Date _1·21·91_

FIGURE 1–6   Grade Kindergarten, boy. Languages: Mien, English

Reflections on the Parent-Teacher Conference

The following comments about the conference between parent and teacher reveal how much it is prized by both participants.

From Parents

I feel that your conferencing format was great. I think it is helpful to the teacher as well as to the child if the teacher knows about a child's interests at home. It also gave me (the parent) a chance to compare my child's school interests with her interests at home.

I enjoyed the conference because I appreciated the careful attention you showed my child and me. I appreciate being a part of the assessment process and am happy to hear that new alternatives are being sought to assess learning . . .

I like the focus being on the child as a person. It's important to know how a child is doing in school, but it's also important for a parent and a teacher to know that kid and to know what makes him tick.

Before [with past conferences] when you go in they're telling you about your kid . . . so I found myself always injecting what I'm telling you now, because I always felt that T. was reacting to what was going on in his home life. I felt like he was doing things for a reason and I don't think the teachers were aware of it.

From Teachers

We used to do parent conferencing where a parent would come in and we would inform them on how their student was doing in the class, how they were doing academically, and they sat and listened, and at the end we'd say, "Do you have any questions?" and sometimes we'd run out of time; they might get one or two questions in. But now we . . . well, it's a two-way street. They're the ones who open up with telling us how they perceive their student, some characteristics of their student. They do most of the talking and we then become the listeners. At the end, we then, together, come up with goals for the student; where we'd like to see them go both socially and academically through the year.

You don't come [to the conference] with a lot of paperwork. You come with your open form that you and the parents are going to fill out together. The preparation was different. It wasn't as time-consuming, I don't feel.

Our district decided to reschedule parent conference times to earlier and later in the year so that all of us could learn about our students from their parents at the outset and parents could review and add to student records (with their portfolios) at year's end.

Examples of What Teachers Say to Parents

The knowledge that parents have about their child's growth and development as learners needs to be tapped by teachers. The following letter shows one way some early primary teachers have gone about inviting parents to school for this important event.

Any School

Any City

Any Date

Dear Parents:

Soon we will be having our regular school conferences to give us time to discuss your child's learning progress thoroughly. You get to share first—you are the expert on your child and your insights will help me plan the best educational program for him or her.

I will ask you to tell me what your child does at home that's important to what we do at school. Some things to think about might be:

1. What are some of your child's favorite stories and rhymes?

2. What kinds of reading does your child enjoy at home? For example, nature magazines, his or her own books, books from school, etc.

3. Is your child aware of print around him or her? For example, on TV, signs, computers, labels on food, etc.

4. Does your child prefer to read or be read to?

5. What opportunities are there for writing at home?

6. What writing do you see your child do at home?

7. What are your child's special interests at home, including favorite toys, games, or TV programs?

I look forward to talking with you soon!

Sincerely,

A2 Student Conference: Record of Discussion Between Student and Teacher

The learning conference is intended to give students an opportunity to talk about themselves as learners. It will also show the teacher what students perceive as their strengths and weaknesses, and what goals and interests they have. As the LR is used by teachers throughout the school, students and their parents can use the goals set in Part A to compare year-to-year achievements and to establish new criteria for measuring success in their own terms.

The value of this conference for students is that it helps them link their world *outside* the school with what they must do for success *in* school. Because the LR will show what and how the student learns throughout the year, in A2 students contribute "baseline data" from which to measure accomplishment. Upper-grade students, especially, need to assess their own experience as readers, writers, and learners and to set the direction for the year's work in these areas. Teachers may want to have older students review the reading and writing scales provided as Appendix A to pinpoint direction during the upcoming year. These scales describe stages of literacy development that both assess student progress and inform instruction.

Timing

At least two conferences of this nature need to take place during the year: one in the first quarter (Section A2) and one in the fourth quarter (Section C2). They can take as long as teachers wish. Generally speaking, fifteen to twenty minutes is enough time to establish rapport and gather useful information for the record.

Procedure

Above all, the conference should be a sharing of information by the student. The teacher meets with each student in a comfortable place in the classroom while the rest of the class is engaged in independent or small-group activities. Or the teacher may schedule the conference during non-class time. With older children, the conferences can be conducted via dialog journal writing. (See the chapter "Classroom Organization and Management" for ways teachers have found to conduct these conferences in the classroom.) The following suggestions may help the teacher plan for these conferences:

1. Explain to the class beforehand about what the teacher and student will be doing so the conference is uninterrupted, except for emergencies.

2. Ask the student to bring a book or a piece of writing to the conference as a way to initiate the conversation.

3. Adapt the conference for students learning English as a second language (e.g., include a peer or sibling interpreter, look at a book in the student's home language).

4. Hold the conference in a place where the student will feel at ease.

5. Invite the student to talk about himself or herself as a learner. (As in the Parent Conference, the teacher may need to ask some prompting or open-ended questions.)

6. Consider both home and school activities involving literacy and learning as appropriate topics for discussion.

7. Consider holding conferences late in the first quarter when students will be more comfortable with the teacher.

8. Share some of the more interesting, confidence-building information from the parent conference as a way to open the student conference.

Examples from the Student-Teacher Conference

Examples of the records of conferences give a clear indication of how students evaluate and reflect on their own learning. They share opinions about the types of books they enjoy reading. They explain where and when they do their best work, and they also articulate areas of weakness.

These conferences give the teacher vital insights into the student as a learner that can be incorporated into classroom activities and then reviewed with the student during the fourth quarter in completing Part C.

Lila's teacher recorded her comments as they conferenced early in the year (Figure 1–7). Her confidence and independence as a sixth-grade monolingual English student are clear, and so is her understanding about her own best way to learn. She faces the challenge of working hard in school and is not dismayed by what there is to learn. She is able to reflect on her abilities, her learning strategies, and her favorite authors.

A2 Record of language/literacy conference with child   (CLR Handbook for teachers K-6, Part A2)

L. says that, "From everything I've heard from my teachers and Mom, I'm over average in reading...Reading is one of my favorite things to do." L. likes mysterys, W. D. Roberts, J. Blume and "Kinda like R. Dahl." She says that A WRINKLE IN TIME was a challenge. When she has trouble with a word or idea, she asks Mom for help. She says, "I always keep Mom informed about what I read."

L. says she likes writing a lot, and has written many poems, some serious and some silly. Her two favorite subjects are reading and writing, though writing takes more time because it is harder. L. says, "I can improve my writing by not getting pressure. If I have time, as long as no one is rushing me, I can do better, I hate deadlines." She says she can work on her careless errors.

Date _____

FIGURE 1–7   Grade Six, girl. Language: English

Carrie's voice is clear in this literacy conference (Figure 1–8). She is able to articulate when and how she learned to read. She sees a relationship between what she can do now that she couldn't do last year. She realizes that people do not improve their reading merely by growing older. She will have to work at it and she's ready.

Carrie is able to set a goal for herself: to learn to read chapter books. Reaching such a goal with her teacher's help will prepare Carrie to set expectations for her own progress and take responsibility for it.

Teachers whose conference summaries appear in this section have listened to their students and recorded significant aspects of what they heard about literacy and learning preferences and prior experiences. When teachers quote the children directly or indirectly, they often get a truer picture of the child into the record. In Figure 1–9, Pam reveals, for example, that she thinks reading is absorbing the author's point of view and reading text correctly. Noting specific titles of books enjoyed helps establish interests and strengths that can be extended in the classroom or at home. Pam's love of reading may lead to more complex literature, for instance, if the teacher knows she's interested in topics explored superficially in her present reading diet.

A2 Record of language/literacy conference with child (CLR Handbook for Teachers K-6, Part A2)

C. says that she likes to read stories and write them. She makes up scary stories and has started a chapter book about the Ghost and Dr. Mad and the Guillermo family. C. has her own books at home that Mom bought her including a set of encyclopedias. She likes to go to the library with her mom. She picks out her own books. C. likes fairy tales especially. She shared a Russian folktale.

Date ___11-13-91___

Published as a component of The California Learning Record. For further information call or write the Center for Language in Learning at 10610 Quail Canyon Road, El Cajon, CA 92021 (619) 443-6320.

FIGURE 1–8   Grade One, girl. Language: English

A2 Record of language/literacy conference with child (CLR Handbook for teachers K-6, Part A2)

P   says reading is understanding and pronouncing the words correctly. She thinks reading is fun and gives her something to do when she has extra time. P   says reading has always been easy for her, but she still reads every day to stay "good." Her favorite kinds of books are chapter books. Her favorite author is Ann M. Martin. THE BABYSITTER CLUB BOOKS. She reads a lot at home and has lots of books at home. She likes to write a lot, especially poems. She feels school is "a good place to learn." Reading is her favorite subject.

Date 9/21/94

FIGURE 1–9   Grade Five, girl. Languages: Spanish, English

Some students will present inaccurate pictures of their literacy development because it does not fit their own expectations. Jason's teacher identified a discrepancy between what Jason said about what he could do and what she had already observed in classroom activities (Figure 1–10). She simply recorded the discrepancy at this time. Later, she found that Jason was very unconfident about his reading ability and relied on his extraordinary skills in talking and drawing to communicate. She then planned opportunities to expand his reading fluency to meet his own expectations. (See pages 36–37 for further data on Jason.)

Alan's (Figure 1–11) teacher learned about Alan's bilingual abilities during the conference. In the fourth grade, Alan switches from Hindi and Punjabi at home, where he is steeped in community languages, to English and the Hardy Boys mysteries. His father supports his learning and obviously is eager for him to succeed in school. The teacher has much information to go on in helping him do so.

Judy, whose recorded conference with the teacher is shown as Figure 1–12, is in a primary language class. Her teacher, who is bilingual in Spanish and English, wrote the conference summary in Spanish first so Judy's

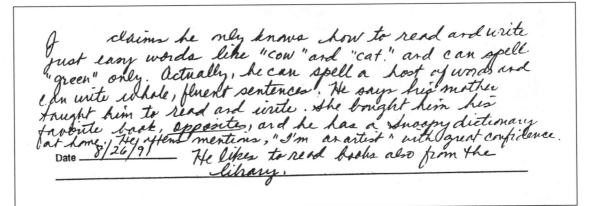

FIGURE 1–10   Grade One, boy. Languages: English, Tagalog

A2 Record of language/literacy conference with child (CLR Handbook for Teachers K–6, Part A2)

According to A. both parents speak Hindi and Punjabi at home. He understands some Hindi but is not as "good" as he once was. He has 1 Hindi book at home and his dad plans to help him learn to read it. He attends Sikh services where he listens to lectors read in the community languages. A.'s favorite books are the Hardy Boys Mysteries and other books he chooses from the neighborhood library. He reads regularly at home at his desk. He plays often with his baby brother and cousins. He prefers to write in pieces rather than stories and will write with his cousin. He shares his writing with his dad on occasion. He prefers to work alone because he has "more concentration."
Date 12-99

FIGURE 1–11   Grade Four, boy. Languages: English, Hindu

Original

"Yo me siento feliz con libros. Me gusta leer mucho, estudiar mucho, escribir cuentos, canciones y poesia hacer reportes de los libros que leo." Ju   trajo 9 libros de la biblioteca escuela, en ingles y espaol Me gusta todo lo que pasa en los libros, tambien a mi papa y mama. Ella dice que ella lee a sus padres y que ellos tambien le leen libros a ella: Expreso que aprehde mucho leyendo y escribiendo, siente que debe de estudiar mucho porque do grande desca ser maestra pero que para serio te aye saber todas las cosas del mundo, para cuando mis alumnos me pregunten algo e gusta leer en espaol e ingles, prefiere hacer lo en espaol porque entiende mas lo que lee y por lo tanto "acabo el libro mas rapido." Le gustan los de ingles porque ma y mas libros de ingles en las bibliotecas. Cuanto leo en ingles y no entiendo algo miro las figuras, peinso un rato y ya entiendo." Le gusta escribir y escriber muy bien, pero solo quiere escribir si alguien (compaeros, maestros, padres) va a leer lo que escribe.

Translation

"I feel happy with books. I like to read a lot, to study a lot, to write tales, songs and poetry, and to write reports about the books I read." Ju   bought 9 books from the school library, both in Spanish and English. "I like everything that goes on in the books, and so do my parents. She said that she reads toher parents and her parents read to her. She expressed that she learns a lot by reading and writing. She feels that she has to study a lot because when she grows older she wants to become a teacher, but in order to do so "I have to study a lot to know everything in the world, to be ready when my students ask me something." She likes to read in Spanish and English although she prefers to read in Spanish because she understands better when she reads and therefore "I finish to read the book faster." She said she likes to read in English too because she can find more books written in English than in Spanish in the library. "When I read in English and I don't understand something I look at the pictures. I think for a while and I understand." She likes to write and she writes very well but she only wants to write if somebody (peers, teachers, parents) is going to read what she writes.

FIGURE 1–12   Grade Two, girl. Languages: Spanish, English

mother could read her child's record. Judy is obviously confident about her literacy skills, which she is beginning to transfer to her reading and writing in English. As evidence, Judy checks books out of the library in both English and Spanish; prefers to read in her primary language as yet in order to read faster (and more, her teacher can conclude); and enjoys support from her parents, who not only get her to a library but read what she writes.

Judy's developing fluency in Spanish, her first language, is a ready asset and a sound base for developing fluency in English. Her parents obviously support development of her bilingual literacy. Judy will need only a little guidance toward more reading and writing in both languages to continue and broaden her literacy.

Hilary Hester's "Stages of English Language Learning," included as Appendix B, is

useful in helping teachers understand how they can build on the prior experiences of readers and writers who are learning to read in two languages.

Topics

Although the following questions may suggest topics for discussion about reading and writing, they should not be used in a rigid question-and-answer format that distracts students from saying what *they* want teachers to know. A good way to start is to say, "I'm going to take notes as we talk today about your learning, especially about your reading and writing, because what you have to say is important to me and I want to remember it."

Here are some suggestions for prompting student description of reading tastes, beliefs about literacy, and experience.

For Knowledge and Understanding, and for the Ability to Reflect

"If someone didn't know anything about reading, how would you describe it to them?"

"What is reading?" "How do you do it?"

"How did you learn to read?" "Who taught you?"

"How old were you when you learned to read?"

For Skills and Strategies

"When is reading hard for you?" "What do you do then?"

"What do you do when you don't know a word?"

"How can you get better at reading?"

"Do you have a favorite book or author that you like to read over and over?"

"How do you choose a book in the library?" "At home?"

For Prior Experience

"Why did you choose these books to show to me today?"

The following prompts can help students discuss writing.

For Knowledge and Understanding, and for Confidence and Independence

"Tell me about what you wrote (or drew)."

"Would you rather write or read?"

"What would you like to learn that would help you with your writing?"

For Skills and Strategies

"Do you ever have trouble deciding on a topic?" "What do you do then?"

"What are your favorite things to write about?"

"Who do you like to share your writing with?" "Do you write letters, stories, or poems to share with someone else?"

"How do you usually get ideas for writing?"

"Do you ever read something and then try to write something like it?"

Reflections on the Student-Teacher Conference

The following reflections, from teachers and students, illustrate the value of this conversation between teachers and students.

From Teachers

Before my first conference, I felt apprehensive . . . about appearing to fumble through it. I chose a child who was very confident as a person and a reader and could key into the conference. I discovered it was really informative and rewarding to interact with E. during the conference. She was thoughtful but quick to answer and seemed genuinely pleased that I

was asking for her opinions, her facts, and her insights into her history as a reader and writer. It was easy to conduct the conference using the questions in the handout!

After the conference I felt more connected to N. as a learner and a person than I felt before. I don't know of another avenue of assessment that could have had as much meaning. . . . I also discovered that writing the information down was important not just for future reference but for clarifying my understanding as well.

From Students

I feel good to talk to someone that I could trust. The conference was a thing that I always wanted to do with a teacher. We talked about reading and writing. But not just that. We talked about other stuff that had to do with my family.

I felt good. It was fun saying all those things. I guess I am a reader. It's fun. I love reading. I love when my mom reads to me. Also, I like when I read to her. I also like *Where's Waldo*.

Putting Part A Together

Examples of discussions between parents and teachers as well as students and teachers help us realize the wealth of experiences that parents provide for their children at home. Teachers see broader pictures of their students than is possible to form in the classroom alone. They view learners as people in their unique worlds. Information about these worlds can then be incorporated, or at least considered, in subsequent teaching.

As the results of the learning conferences held by the teacher with Miguel and his mother indicate, for instance, much valuable information is revealed in the Part A section of the LR. Note especially in the record shown as Figure 1–13 just how much can already be identified about Miguel's prior literacy experiences and the support he has at home. Experience has taught him that he can learn, which in turn has made him confident to learn more. The teacher's responsibility will be to build on the literacy Miguel has brought to school.

The Learning Record (Elementary)

Adapted with permission from the Primary Language Record (PLR), Developed and copyrighted by the Centre for Language in Primary Education, Webber Row Teacher's Centre, Webber Row, London SE1 8QW, in 1988 and distributed in the U.S. by Heinemann Educational Books, Inc. ISBN 0-435-08519-8

School _____ Teacher _____ School Year _____

Name _____ Grade Level __1__ Birth Date _____

Boy/Girl __Boy__

Languages understood	Languages read	Languages spoken	Languages written
Spanish, English	Spanish, some English	Spanish, English	Spanish

Details of any aspect of hearing, vision, or coordination affecting the child's language/literacy. Give the source and date of this information.	Names of staff involved with child's development.

PART A To be completed during the first quarter

A1 Record of discussion between child's parent(s) and class teacher (CLR Handbook for teachers K-6, Part A)

His mother says that she didn't do anything to prepare him to read. Her son is persistent—he asks a lot of questions when he wants to know something. She thinks that his older cousin taught him to read playing "school." She reads with him every night and they discuss what was read. He always asks "What does it say here?" In pre-school he could write his first and last name. His teacher told her that he's bright. She didn't know he could read until one evening he told her—"Mom, this says. . . ." and he read. He tells her that when he grows up he is going to be the President of the United States. He draws and writes all day.

Signed Parent(s) _____ Teacher _____

Date _____

A2 Record of language/literacy conference with child (CLR Handbook for teachers K-6, Part A2)

He likes to play with the cars that Santa Claus brought him. He has races with his cars. He also likes to draw many things. His mother always reads to him, especially before he goes to sleep. He knows how to read because one day he wanted to read and he looked, looked and looked at books and then he read a book. Then he began to read. He read by himself. Now he likes to read. Reading is studying. He can write stories. He writes at home on a paper.

Date _____

Published as a component of The Learning Record Assessment System. For further information, call or write the Center for Language in Learning, at 10610 Quail Canyon Road, El Cajon, CA 92021 (619) 443-6320. Computer application created by Intelligent Solutions, © 1995 by Saul Krimsly.

FIGURE 1–13   Grade One, boy. Languages: Spanish, English

Documenting Student Learning

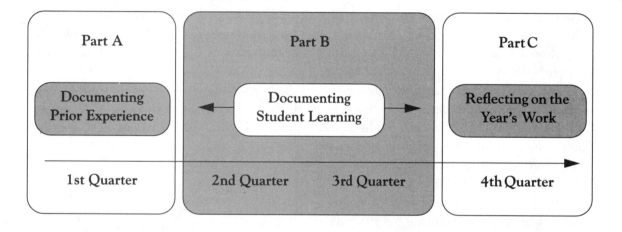

Part A	Part B	Part C
Documenting Prior Experience	← **Documenting Student Learning** →	**Reflecting on the Year's Work**
1st Quarter	2nd Quarter 3rd Quarter	4th Quarter

In Part B, teachers observe students as they work on classroom tasks and course projects. They look for evidence of student progress and document when and how they collected the information. Toward the end of the third quarter, teachers summarize the evidence of achievement in terms of goals set in the first quarter.

What teachers learned about each student during the first quarter of the year in Part A's conferences with parents and students provides the context for observing and sampling student work over the rest of the year. What students can do outside the classroom, they can, with teachers' help, relate to new learning experiences at school. What they have indicated experience and interest in can be tapped to improve the authenticity of classroom activities.

The five dimensions of learning discussed on page 3 provide a framework for describing student progress in Part B. Teachers will be able to tell from the initial parent and student conferences in Part A the degree of *confidence and independence* students have in learning in specific areas of the curriculum. In addition, student *experience* with subject area ideas and processes as well as the extent of their grasp of *strategies* and subject matter *knowledge and understanding* can be preliminarily assessed with Part A. The conversation documented in A2 will give teachers insights into the students' abilities to *reflect* on their own learning. Part A and Part B both supply information from which to gather evidence that students are adding to their prior knowledge and skills—that is, that they are learning.

This section begins with an overview of Part B: its purpose in the yearlong assessment of student learning and the way one teacher has completed this section of the LR. To illustrate what one teacher observed and concluded about one student's growth during the first three quarters of one year, the complete data collection and summary section, which comprise Part B, is provided first (Figures 2–2 through 2–11). The student is James; he is in Grade 2 and is monolingual English. Readers should refer to copies of both the LR and the Data Collection Form (at the end of this handbook) as they use this part of the handbook, so they can keep track of how the forms work together.

Following the overview of Part B, the chapter is divided into Talking and Listening (B1), Reading (B2), and Writing (B3), to provide more examples of how teachers have completed both the Data Collection Form and the corresponding summary interpretation of the data in Part B of the LR. There are detailed examples and suggestions for making observations, collecting student work, and accounting for students' progress.

Overview of Part B of the Learning Record

Purposes and Procedures

Part B is completed near the end of the third quarter of the year. (Part C will briefly update this part during the fourth quarter to give the full year's picture.) It is divided into three sections:

B1: Talking and Listening

B2: Reading

B3: Writing

The purpose of the data collection is to capture what the students show they can do

relevant to learning goals as they engage in classroom tasks and accumulate evidence of their progress in portfolios of work. The purpose of Part B is to make sense of the notes and work samples the teacher and the student have collected all year.

Although oral and written language are separated in the LR forms, the modes nevertheless interrelate in the normal context of the classroom as they reveal what students discuss or present orally, what they read and understand, what they write and make understandable. The use of language in all subject areas is a fundamental aspect of schooling, necessary if the student is to make sense of new understandings. Figure 2–1 shows the overall view of how information from students about their learning—their reading, writing, and oral discussions and presentations—contributes data to students' records and is informed by the use of the

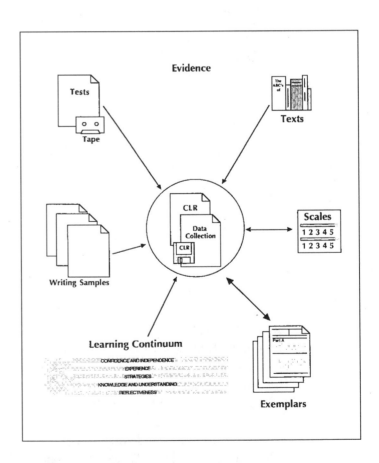

FIGURE 2–1   The Learning Record Assessment System: Classroom

Learning Dimensions, the scales and exemplars of records from other students. The scales and the exemplars are, in turn, interpreted by teachers and their students.

Part B distills what is documented in the data collection section of the LR. In it, teachers summarize "for the record" the evidence they and their students have collected of language and literacy development, and they also describe the learning experiences that have helped or might help students continue to progress. No conclusion is made about the student's performance without supporting evidence. All conclusions describe what the student *can* do. Three pieces of information about yearly progress thus far go into the Part B summaries:

∎ What has been learned?
∎ What might next be learned?
∎ What learning contexts seem most effective?

Example of One Complete Record

James's teacher writes in B1, shown as Figure 2–3, her summary of observations and samples of his work through the first three quarters of the year. She notes that he has participated actively and collaboratively during group share times in class. She notes this behavior as an aspect of oral language development as well as a social skill to increase the chances that James will continue to build on this strength. She knows his parents value his ability in this area because the father mentioned it in the parent interview for Part A. (See Figure 2–2 for the parent and child conference summaries on James's record.)

In the B2 section of the form, the teacher summarizes J.'s growth in reading. As shown in Figure 2–3, she refers to specific samples of his work and and the strategies he has demonstrated. She notes in the continuation of B2 shown in Figure 2–4 that sitting

PART A To be completed during the first quarter

A1 Record of discussion between child's parent(s) and class teacher   (CLR Handbook for teachers K-6, Part A)

J. has set himself a goal to read three hours a week. He reads in the morning and at night. Mom notices that he doesn't move his mouth when he reads anymore. He loves T.V. He likes to make and build things. J. is very creative. He likes to draw. He enjoys puzzles and games. He is patient. J. will tell his parents they are doing a good job. He makes a lot of choices for himself.

Goal—(dad) reading; social skills.

Signed Parent(s) _____   Teacher _____

Date 10/11/93 _____

A2 Record of language/literacy conference with child   (CLR Handbook for teachers K-6, Part A2)

"I like reading—a lot. At least certain books. I like Bill Peet books a lot because his pictures are so good and the words rhyme (I think that's hard to do). He writes great stories about animals." J. likes animal books. He learned how to read when his sister was practicing spelling—then he read bigger and bigger books, and chapter books. J. sounds out words and skips words. "I can usually get them." "I like writing a lot." "I think of animals and problems, that's where the ideas come from for writing." J. comes up with the title, characters and problem before he writes a story. He gets ideas for writing from group share. J. feels more comfortable than nervous when he shares. Drawing animals is his favorite subject—he wants to be better at drawing faces.

Date _____

FIGURE 2–2   Grade Two, boy. Language: English

31

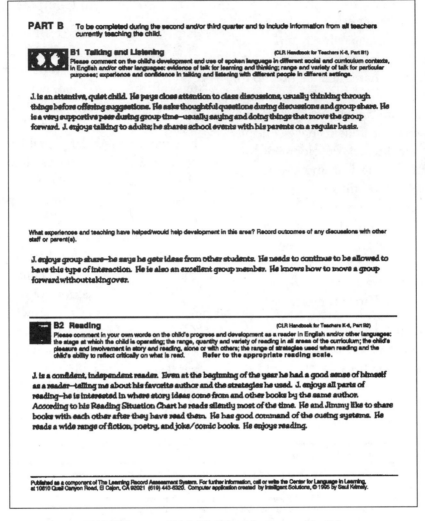

FIGURE 2–3   Grade Two, boy. Language: English

next to someone as he reads is a helpful strategy for James She also places him on Reading Scale 1 at this time as a Fluent Reader (4). (This placement is written at the top of Part C, so that teacher, parent, and student can refer to it easily as they update the LR in the final quarter of the year.)

James's ability to write in many different situations is one of the strengths the teacher notes in B3 shown in Figure 2–4. That she connects his reading to his writing also resonates with what he and his parents had told her in A2.

Data Collection: Observing and Documenting Learning

Before teachers can compose the summaries for Part B, they need evidence for their con-

clusions. Teacher conclusions or judgments about student achievement are based on information collected and interpreted throughout the year. The information includes observation notes and actual work samples. To make the evidence explicit and open to all who have a stake in the student's progress—parents, other teachers, the student—the LR Data Collection Form helps teachers assemble the evidence they need for the annual summaries of achievement. Most important, the form also helps them monitor growth so they can provide specific learning opportunities during the year.

On the first page of the Data Collection Form, James's teacher notes his oral capabilities during class share times. The matrix at the top of the form, shown as Figure 2–5,

(B2 continued)

What experiences and teaching have helped/would help development in this area? Record outcomes of any discussions with other staff or parent(s).

J. still enjoys having stories read aloud and being able to sit next to someone when he reads. He enjoys a wide range of books.

B3 Writing (CLR Handbook for Teachers K-6, Part B2)
Please comment on the child's progress and development as a writer in English and/or other languages: the degree of confidence and independence as a writer; the range, quantity and variety of writing in all areas of the curriculum; the child's pleasure and involvement in writing, both narrative and non-narrative, alone and in collaboration with others; the influence of reading on the child's writing; growing understanding of written language, its convention and spelling.

J. is an avid writer. He writes at home and at school. He works out story ideas in his head before he starts writing. J's strong reading skills are apparent in the type of detailed stories he writes. He is attempting dialogue. J. has a good handle on mechanics. He can write to a prompt as well as determining his own topics in Writing Workshop.

What experiences and teaching have helped/would help development in this area? Record outcomes of any discussions with other staff or parent(s).

J. continues to struggle with conventional spelling. We have been working on using other resources (dictionary). J. should try other types of writing besides story.

Signed: Classroom Teacher _____ Date _____
Other Staff Contributor(s) _____ Date _____

Published as a component of The Learning Record Assessment System. For further information, call or write the Center for Language in Learning, at 10610 Quail Canyon Road, El Cajon, CA 92021 (619) 443-6320. Computer application created by Intelligent Solutions, © 1995 by Saul Krimsly.

FIGURE 2–4   Grade Two, boy. Language: English

however, indicates that she has observed his talk and listening only with an adult present. To document his ability to communicate more broadly, the teacher overlooked the need to show that James can engage in collaborative conversation with his peers or with younger children. Since his mother shared in A1 that he has a history of decision making at home and his contributions to class discussions are thoughtful, the teacher can assume the conversational ability, but she has not proved it. She also lacks evidence that he can use language to explore as-yet-unformulated ideas, the kind of language that is best done with a friendly peer.

The rest of the Data Collection Form is devoted to collecting evidence of literacy. On the second page, Figure 2–6, the teacher has recorded her observations regarding James's ability in reading second-grade material. She recorded evidence from September to April that he was understanding a variety of kinds of texts.

James's thoughtful approach to writing is apparent in the observations in Figure 2–6. He listens attentively to others when they share their writing, asks pertinent questions, and gives contextual information when he shares his own work.

The teacher also has documented demonstrations of his ability to compose text that can be understood by others, thereby introducing the idea that writing is to be read, and not just by the teacher. James's ability to help a group move forward is noted in the December observation. The

Data Collection   (The Learning Record, Elementary)

Name: J   Grade Level: 2

1. Talking & Listening: observation notes

The space below is for recording examples of the child's developing use of talk for learning and for interacting with others in English and/or other languages.

Include different kinds of talk (e.g., planning an event, solving a problem, expressing a point of view or feeling, reporting on the results of an investigation, telling a story...).

Note the child's experience and confidence in handling social dimensions of talk (e.g., initiating a discussion, listening to another contribution, qualifying former ideas, encouraging others...).

The matrix sets out some possible contexts for observing talk and listening. It may be useful for addressing reading or writing development as well. Observations made in the space below can be plotted on the matrix to record the range of social and curriculum contexts sampled.

(CLR Handbook for Teachers K-6, Part B)

LEARNING CONTEXTS	SOCIAL CONTEXTS				
	pair	small group	child with adult	small or large group with adult	
collaborative reading and writing activities				XXX	
play, dramatic play, drama & storying			X		
environmental studies & historical research					
math & science investigations					
design, construction, crafts & arts projects			XX		

Attach additional pages as necessary

Dates	Observations and their contexts
9/27	J. shared a joke book during group share. He read a few jokes aloud to the class.
10/93	J. brought in an audio tape of a story he wrote at home—he told me there were some mistakes.
11/30	J. asking thoughtful questions during R.W. group share.
1/26	During Part A J. seemed very comfortable talking to me. He gave long elaborate answers—he seemed happy and excited while he talked.
2/15	When I read PIGGYBOOK, J. said "They're in a happy mood—she's in a sad mood. The lady in the picture is gone."
5/94	J. was interviewed by a researcher from U.C.L.A. He was comfortable talking with her about his work. He shared strong opinions about his work.

Published as a component of The Learning Record Assessment System. For further information, call or write the Center for Language in Learning, at 10610 Quail Canyon Road, El Cajon, CA 92021 (619) 443-6320. Computer application created by Intelligent Solutions. © 1995 by Saul Krimsly.

FIGURE 2–5   Grade Two, boy. Language: English

teacher has designed a reading log, a simplified reading sampling form, an "Oral Reading Self-Evaluation" form, and a "Reading Situation" sheet to help James begin to keep track of his own reading experience for the LR. (See Figure 2–7.)

The last two pages of the Data Collection Form provide for comparative analyses of three reading samples (page 3) and three writing samples (page 4). James's teacher has collected the reading and writing samples to provide a closer look at his literacy than is possible in her more informal observations. She selected samples in December, March, and early June to examine. Together with what she knows from James's parents and James himself, and from her own documented observations, the samples inform her instruction.

James's three reading samples (Figure 2–8) show areas of growth. He has improved his fluency as shown by the development of his ability to use all cueing systems. He expects text to make sense and he persists until it does; he tracks visually, using punctuation as a clue to meaning. He comprehends grade-level text and, as shown in the *Oliver Button* sample used as an abbreviated miscue analysis, he can cite the text's relevance to his own life. Still consolidating his strategies, he seems ready at each sampling time to tackle more complex text. One wishes that the teacher had suggested more concretely just what kind of support he needs to read novels and nonfiction. (See page 66 for specific suggestions.) But, since she has wisely begun to require her students, even at Grade 2, to reflect on their learning by involving them in

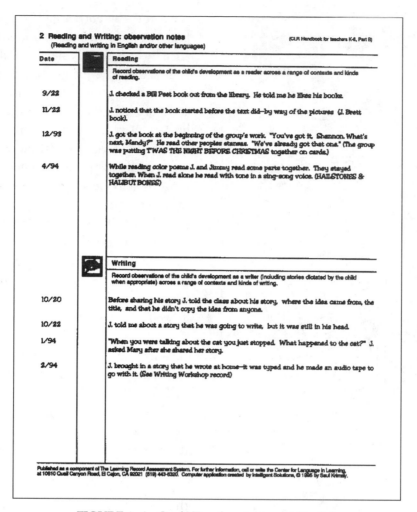

FIGURE 2–6 Grade Two, boy. Language: English

self-assessment, James himself may be able to take the recommendation to heart. As he says in the end of the year interview for Part C, "I think I am going to read a novl. I lirnd how to read hder wrds."

The boxes on the Reading Sample page of the Data Collection Form as well as on the Writing Sample page are designed to collect quick responses to the "prompts" in the left-hand column on each page. The prompts themselves are brief reminders to the teacher and the student of some key questions to ask of the reading or writing sample regarding the reading strategies being applied in different contexts, and the learning opportunities that the student needs to progress. Selections from James's portfolio, shown as Figure 2–9, provide evidence of the judgments his teacher has made.

The three writing samples (noted in Figure 2–10) show that James can express himself effectively in a broad range of writing purposes—from an assigned topic, to a self-conceived story drafted over time, to an essay ("Dear Reader" letter) written in collaboration with a partner. The fact that the prompt on the side of the form asks for a holistic or "overall impression" of the work from the points of view of the teacher and the student is important to students' growing understanding about the need to address an ever-widening audience for their work.

Finally, the sampling form calls for a judgment about the student's current status as a writer and the resources needed to support his or her further development. To encourage self-evaluation, James's teacher has developed a record-keeping sheet for the

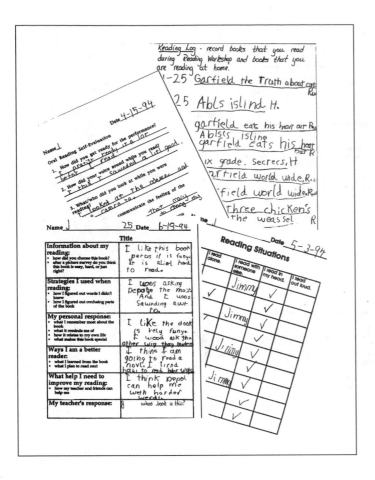

FIGURE 2–7

writing projects that develop over time. This form and selections from his portfolio to corroborate the judgments on the Writing Sample sheet are shown as Figure 2–11.

The reading and writing scales James's teacher used to analyze his literacy achievement are included as Appendix A. Another scale, devised by Hilary Hester for use in Great Britain, can be used to assess the learning of English by speakers of another language. It is included as Appendix B.

After this overview of Part B, using James's record, the rest of this section is devoted to examples of how other teachers have completed this section of the LR for their students.

Talking and Listening

The importance of oral language in learning is often undervalued. Both talking and listening

cut across the curriculum, through a child's investigations and observations in math, science, history/social science, and literature—and across the language modes, through talking with others in reading and writing activities designed to promote thoughtful literacy. Within the classroom contexts, the quality and range of oral language opportunities will significantly affect the child's progress and development as a talker, listener, and learner. Talking and listening in school can mean both formal or public speaking and informal or private speech. Most important for teachers, parents, and children to know is that opportunity for oral language use across a full range of informal as well as formal contexts must be afforded throughout the day.

How children use language to explore experience and how they express what they understand is at the crux of learning—both for them and for their teachers. The students must incorporate what they are learning in their own terms, adding it to what they already know; their teachers must recognize that what students say is a window into what they are thinking. Student talking and listening behaviors can be captured by an observing teacher as students work in collaborative groups or in pairs, as they carry out self-initiated activities, engage in imaginative play, share their daily work, or relate experiences from home. The classroom environment that provides such contexts for learning encourages students to talk with others as they read literature and textbooks or write in response to a problem-solving activity. While it is sometimes difficult to observe and document the use of talk and listening, teachers have found that paying attention to student progress in oral expression helps them better understand what students can do.

The observations of Jason, a first-grade boy whose first language is Tagalog, reveal a range of learning experiences and oral language development strategies. The teacher's notes depict a student with a finely tuned ear

3 Reading Samples (Reading in English and/or other languages) To include reading aloud and reading silently			(CLR Handbook for teachers K-6, Part II)
Dates	12/2	3/4	6/1
Title or book/text (literary or information)	TATTLING	OLIVER BUTTON	THE SUPRISE PARTY
Known/unknown text	Known	Unknown	Known
Sampling procedure used: informal assessment/ running record/ miscue analysis	Informal Read aloud	Miscue	Informal
Overall impression of the child's reading: • confidence and degree of independence • involvement in the book/text • the way in which the child reads the text aloud	J. is a confident and self-assured reader.	J. is unaffected by my presence or the miscue. He is an independent reader.	J. is a confident reader.
Strategies used when reading aloud: • drawing on previous experience to make sense of the book/text • playing at reading • using book language • reading the pictures • focusing on print (directionality, 1:1 correspondence, recognition of certain words) • using semantic, syntactic and graphophonic cues • predicting • self-correcting • using several strategies or over-dependence on one	J. tracks visually—his voice is monotone—pace is choppy. J. self-corrects as needed. He worked through unfamiliar words. Cueing systems not outwardly apparent. He had no stops.	J. tracks visually. He chunks phrases and notices punctuation. He is using all cueing systems—repetition omission and substitutions—he doesn't correct all miscues.	J. knew when his miscues didn't make sense. He tracks visually. J. works through text—rereading and hesitating.
Child's response to the book/text: • personal response • critical response (understanding, evaluating, appreciating wider meanings)	"It's telling kids that tattling isn't good."	"He likes to do girls' stuff. I think that's O.K. I like to do girls' stuff like that—I don't like to do rough stuff."	J. thinks he has the book at home. J. told me about the book—concise summary.
What this sample shows about the child's development as a reader. **Experiences/support needed to further development.**	J. should be moving into non-fiction or more challenging fiction.	I'd like to see J. tackle a novel or some non-fiction.	J. continues to read picture books. He needs support to move into non-fiction and novels.

* Early indicators that the child is moving into reading   Please attach text samples described on this sheet.

Published as a component of The Learning Record Assessment System. For further information, call or write the Center for Language in Learning, at 10610 Quail Canyon Road, El Cajon, CA 92021 (619) 443-6320. Computer application created by Intelligent Solutions. © 1995 by Saul Krimsly.

FIGURE 2–8   Grade Two, boy. Language: English

who often tries out the phrasing and vocabulary of adults with great confidence, and even looks at fine distinctions between song and the spoken word. The teacher has incorporated the audiotaped information sampled in Figure 2–12 with what she has overheard in other classroom situations.

Implicit in the teacher's notes in Figure 2–13 are the kinds of activities the teacher provides. Because the activities support independent learning, she can observe the student applying knowledge, skills, and strategies as well as exhibiting confidence as a learner. Jason has opportunities to use a computer, build a train out of Unifix cubes, and lead an alphabet drill with a group of his peers.

Jason's teacher has utilized the matrix at the top of the Data Collection Form to ana-

lyze her observations. The matrix helps teachers provide a variety of contexts for talking and listening. For example, the teacher might want to arrange for Jason to work in a large-group situation. Is he more reserved in these situations or has she just missed hearing him in this more formal setting? The matrix helps her see where the gaps are in Jason's oral language experience.

The teacher uses her observation notes about Jason's oral language development to complete a summary of what she knows of his learning across a spectrum of social and learning contexts. The summary, B1, shown as Figure 2–14, reveals that six-year-old Jason's talking and listening in two languages is unusually skillful. His skills in this area, however, have sometimes been stymied by his lack of "diplomacy," as when he called

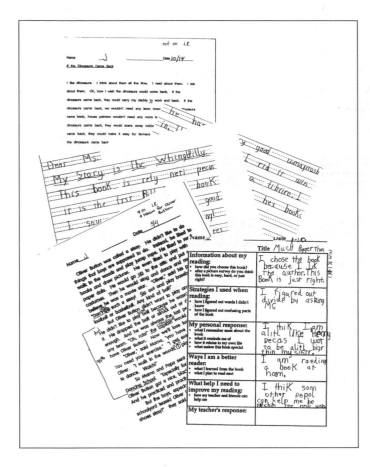

FIGURE 2–9

someone else's work "ugly." The teacher records the event as an occasion for him to know more about talking and listening, and in so doing promotes further development.

One reading specialist learning to use the LR observed, "It's impossible to watch and think about how a particular child is learning to read and write and talk about things of importance to him without coming to respect the determination and courage that he brings to his work." This is certainly the case with Gina, Figure 2–15, who demonstrates her confidence in her speaking ability by voluntarily participating in activities such as reader's theater and author's chair. The confidence enables her to reflect critically on her performance when she hears her own recorded voice. Her teacher, in response, plans more language activities that allow Gina to use her talking and listening purposefully in authentic contexts.

In Figure 2–16, Alex's teacher has documented several of Alex's language experiences as they occurred during the year, from mid-November to the end of February, and has then summarized this information in terms of his progress for B1. The teacher notes in the summary that she has worked with Alex for two years, so her analysis is especially comprehensive. She also discusses his participation in the school's special education program ("RST and Sp[eech] & Lang[uage]") and has, consequently, incorporated quotes from Alex's teacher in that program, indicating that they work together to see that Alex succeeds. This practice exemplifies the way the LR can encourage collaboration among site staff on behalf of all students, especially those with special needs.

Reading

It hardly needs to be said that children learn according to their own sequences, the pace and manner influenced by prior experience, interests, and self-definition of themselves as learners. Using the LR's scales as references for assessing literacy proficiency, teachers can help their students use what they already know to become experienced readers and writers. When teachers know what and how students learn they can provide relevant opportunities to learn more with appropriate books and activities.

It may be that some children need more knowledge of letter sounds or perhaps they lack the confidence to risk error. Maybe a student can read a story but not a math problem. It may be that the male student sees reading as effeminate or considers the texts offered in school profane or too "white" or babyish. Maybe the child is learning English as a second language and needs something to read in the home language. One-size assessments definitely do not apply to all learners, so the Learning Record Assessment System™ follows the child in order to inform the instructional program.

4 Writing Samples (Writing in English and/or other languages)
Writing to include children's earliest attempts at writing

Dates	9/93	2/94	5/94
Contexts and background information about the writing • how the writing arose • how the child went about the writing • whether the child was writing alone or with others • whether the writing was discussed with anyone while the child was working on it • the kind of writing (e.g., list, letter, story, poem, personal writing, information writing) • complete piece of work/extract	Favorite Pet -assigned topic about Favorite Pet -brainstormed as a class -students could discuss writing as they worked -extended time given	The Two Eagles -a Writing Workshop selection -J. got the idea from Paul -took a few weeks to write this story	Important Page -students read the IMPORTANT BOOK -then wrote their own page -worked alone and in pairs -partner helped with editing and brainstorming -rough draft was done prior to final copy
Child's own response to the writing.		J. likes this story because it's long, it's funny, and it has detailed pictures.	Justin's "Dear Reader" letter says this is the best piece in his portfolio.
Teacher's response: • to the content of the writing • to the child's ability to handle this particular kind of writing • overall impressions	J. was able to respond well to the prompt. He wrote in long complex sentences that followed each other well. He used descriptive language.	J. is comfortable writing and illustrating long stories with many details. He has a strong sense of what he wants his story to come out like.	J. is a confident writer. He is able to work with a peer to edit his work. He was able to incorporate his artwork into this assignment.
Development of spelling and conventions of writing.	Very neat. Printing, periods and caps present. Spelling is invented and conventional.	J. has a handle on caps and periods. Most high frequency words are spelled correctly—other words are phonetic.	J. is a phonetic speller. He is learning to use a dictionary. He is consistent with caps and periods.
What this writing shows about the child's development as a writer • how it fits into the range of the child's previous writing • experience/support needed to further development	Invented spelling is consistent. J. showed his ability to construct ideas and thought. We need to work on spelling.	J. is learning to use a dictionary. I would like to see him try another type of writing.	J. is an imaginative writer. He will need some support as he moves into writing non-fiction.

Please attach the writing with this sample sheet.

Published as a component of The Learning Record Assessment System. For further information, call or write the Center for Language in Learning, at 10610 Quail Canyon Road, El Cajon, CA 92021 (619) 443-6320. Computer application created by Intelligent Solutions, © 1995 by Saul Krimsly.

FIGURE 2–10   Grade Two, boy. Language: English

What Is Reading Anyway? And What Does Its Definition Mean for Assessment?

One of education's longest (and loudest) debates has been over how to teach people to read. It is always a contentious issue with polarized opinions. For the most part, the debate has been argued on the basis of what the teacher does or should do to teach reading, and only secondarily, and superficially, on what the student can do. Further, learning to read has often been regarded as the province of early primary teachers with upper elementary, middle, and high school teachers absolved of the responsibility for seeing that their students reach high levels of literacy.

Classroom practices in learning to read are heavily influenced by what teachers and their publics believe reading to be, and their beliefs, in turn, determine what counts as reading. What counts is, unfortunately, often only what parts of reading can be easily and quickly assessed, what scores can be aggregated and disaggregated, and what information can be disseminated to a public growing more and more jaded about the schools' effectiveness in teaching what they perceive as the most rudimentary of skills.

Two Definitions of Reading

Following are two very different definitions of reading and their implications for teaching, learning, and assessing reading performance in school:

1. Some say reading is a linear matter of receiving a written message from an author. Emerging readers, therefore, should focus on fluent and accurate recognition of words by

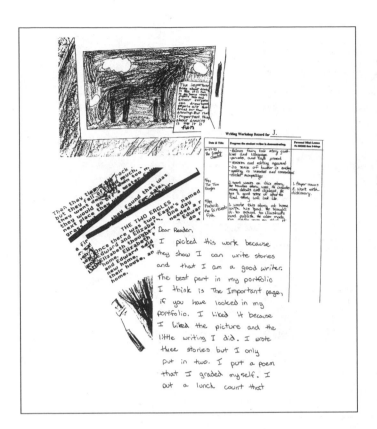

FIGURE 2–11

OVERHEARING STUDENT TALK

The use of an audiopack—a small tape recorder inside a "fanny pack," which straps around a student's waist with an auxiliary clip-on microphone—provides teacher with one more way to "kidwatch." They can overhear the student in a variety of informal learning contexts as he or she works on projects. In the following transcript, J____, a first grader, reveals his oral language skills as he works his way about the classroom during an independent learning period.

Location on Tape	Selected Quotations from Tape
82	"Look at a question mark here. I mean, that—uh—comma like that."
110	"Mrs. M., I'm making my own book. Can I make something for you? I can make it for you. It's easy to me."
120	"I'm gonna be your friend. Come on. I'm gonna make you one. Then I'll give you it. Thank you."
151	"I'm gonna copy it for you. You better not tell a secret to him. You must tell it to me....Yes...."
160	"A...., I'll write this to you. Huh? You like it?"

See Page 38 for the way J 's teacher used the information gathered on the audiotape to help her describe what he is learning

FIGURE 2–12   Grade One, boy. Languages: Tagalog, English

systematically practicing letter-sound combinations in "decodable" books constructed strictly for that purpose. Once they memorize the sounds of letters for automatic retrieval, it is argued, these readers will be able to unlock the thoughts of the author. Those who hold with this definition of reading believe, therefore, that assessment in the primary grades should focus on tests of pronunciation words, in lists or in connected but vocabulary-controlled or grade-leveled texts. Upper-grade students are assumed to be able to read words and, therefore, they are assessed for their ability to "uncover" what the authors of given texts say and mean.
2. Others contend that reading is making sense of the experiences represented in connected or whole texts—with the best material that is found in real books written by authors who not only have something to say but who say it well. Reading, in this sense, engages those just learning the process as well as those who can use the process in creating the meanings that reside in stories,

Data Collection (California Learning Record, Elementary) Attach extra pages where needed

Name: Grade Level:

1 Talking & Listening: diary of observations

The diary below is for recording examples of the child's developing use of talk for learning and for interacting with others in English and/ other languages.

Include different kinds of talk (e.g. planning an event, solving a problem, expressing a point of view or feelings, reporting on the results of an investigation, telling a story...)

Note the child's experience and confidence in handling social dimensions of talk (e.g. initiating a discussion, listening to another contribution, qualifying former ideas, encouraging others...)

The matrix sets out some possible contexts for observing talk and listening. Observations made in the diary are plotted on the matrix to record the range of social and curriculum contexts sampled.

LEARNING CONTEXTS	pair	small group	child with adult	small/large group with adult	variety of indivduals
collaborative reading and writing activities	8/23	9/10			
play, dramatic play, drama & storying		12/10			
environmental studies & historical research					
math & science investigations	9/9				
design, construction, craft & arts projects	7/29				
audiotape					4/7
writing	4/14				
conference			4/14		

Dates	Observations and their contexts
7/29	collaborated with Reginald on a unifix train. "The train is going through the cave."
9/9	working with Madarne at the computer—came running up to me: "I can't believe it! I can't believe it! He said, 'one-two-three-four-five-six !'" (M. just arrived from Spain and speaks little English).
11/7	wearing the audiotape fanny pack: Greetings & negotiations with many students. "What are you doing? Excuse me, Hi! Can I make something for you? I'm gonna be your friend. You like it?"
12/10	organized a learning group—using flash cards "Who gots the letter "C"?"

Adapted with permission from the Primary Language Record (PLR), developed and copyrighted by the Centre for Language in Primary Education, Webber Row Teachers' Centre, Webber Row, London SE1 8QW, in 1988 and distributed in the U.S. by Heinemann Educational Books, Inc. ISBN 0-435-08516-6

FIGURE 2–13   Grade One, boy. Languages: Tagalog, English

PART B To be completed during the second and/or third quarter and to include information from
all teachers currently teaching the child.

Child as a language user (one or more languages)

Teachers may want to refer to the Bilingual Education Handbook, published by and available from the California
Department of Education, ISBN 0-8011-0890-X, in completing each section of the record.

B1 Talking and listening
Please comment on the child's development and use of spoken language in different social and curriculum
contexts, in English and/or other languages: evidence of talk for learning and thinking; range and variety of talk for
particular purposes; experience and confidence in talking and listening with different people in different settings.

J. is very social and understands the inner workings of language for appealing, thinking, and making deals as evidenced by such comments of his like, "Excuse me. Hi! Can I make something for you? I'm gonna be your friend." (his way of curry favor) You like it?" He has a very large vocabulary and uses words like "constellation" and "reception." He is highly attuned to new words and always is the first to ask their meaning. He is also sensitive to others' acquisition of English as when he excitedly yelled, "I can't believe it!" when a new student spoke his first words in English.

What experiences and teaching have helped/would help development in this area? Record outcomes of any discussion with other staff or parent(s).

I encourage J. as a model for other children — I praise his astute knowledge of words — and appeal to his social sense of language in being thoughtful of others. After calling someone else's work "ugly," we discussed how words can hurt people's feelings. He asked, "Then next time I think something is ugly, should I say, 'Oh, that's very nice?'" We discussed the importance of diplomacy vs. lying or being too blunt. It is evident that the adults in his family speak frankly with J., not underestimating his grasp of words, and I try to follow suit in the classroom.

FIGURE 2–14   Grade One, boy. Languages: Tagalog, English

B1 Talking and listening
Please comment on the child's development and use of spoken language in different social and curriculum
contexts, in English and/or other languages: evidence of talk for learning and thinking; range and variety of talk for
particular purposes; experience and confidence in talking and listening with different people in different settings.

G speaks Vietnamese and some English at home. In class, she speaks in both large and small group settings as well as individually with fellow students and teachers. She participates in reader's and author's chair and volunteers to answer questions in large group discussions. She feels comfortable asking for help when she needs help. Likes to practice reading into tape recorder but as she listens to the playback says, "It isn't good reading." She picks up vocabulary from books as she rereads them. Growing use of English vocabulary, especially nouns. Limited use of articles like of, an, a.

What experiences and teaching have helped/would help development in this area? Record outcomes of any discussion with other staff or parent(s).

Opportunities to work in small group projects that require discussion. Hands-on activities with small group or partner to hear English spoken in context of use of read objects. Language Experience activities.

FIGURE 2–15   Grade Two, girl. Languages: Vietnamese, English

Data Collection (California Learning Record, Elementary)   Attach extra pages where needed

Name: Grade Level: 3rd

1. Talking & Listening: observation notes

The space below is for recording examples of the child's developing use of talk for learning and for interacting with others in English and/or other languages.

Include different kinds of talk (e.g., planning an event, solving a problem, expressing a point of view or feeling, reporting on the results of an investigation, telling a story...)

Note the child's experience and confidence in handling social dimensions of talk (e.g., initiating a discussion, listening to another contribution, qualifying former ideas, encouraging others...)

The matrix sets out some possible contexts for observing talk and listening. It may be useful for addressing reading or writing development as well. Observations made in the space below can be plotted on the matrix to record the range of social and curriculum contexts sampled.

(CLR Handbook for Teachers K-6, Part B)

LEARNING CONTEXTS	SOCIAL CONTEXTS				
	pair	small group	child with adult	small or large group with adult	To the class
collaborative reading and writing activities	2-26-97			11-13-96	
play, dramatic play, drama & storying					1-27-97
environmental studies & historical research					
math & science investigations					
design, construction, crafts & arts projects					
Writing expla. to teacher	11-26-97				

Dates	Observations and their contexts
11-13-96	In discussing read aloud book with class, teacher gave several descriptors of the characters behavior, asked, "What would you call what the truck driver was doing?" A. raised his hand, and said,"ignore, he was acting like he was not paying attention to the boy."
11-26-96	A. Came to teacher and explained, "See, I erased the period and added some more words, now the sentence is longer--I put the period her after the new words." and then read completed sentence to teacher.
1-27-97	A. volunteered to recite a poem from the poetry folder by memory. He spoke clearly, confidently, easy to hear voice.
2-26-97	Peer turned to A. and asked "Does it matter what color?" asking about finding a letter in the "Making of Words" spelling activity. A. answered, " There are no a's on white, only on pink, remember they are the vowels."

FIGURE 2–16   Grade Three, boy. Language: English

essays, books, poems. Meaning emerges as the reader participates in a range of set tasks and self-initiated activities appropriate to the stage of development the reader has reached. Assessment in this case focuses on the ability of students to make sense of different kinds of texts by bringing prior knowledge and experiences to bear on whatever they read. Because readers possess many different bodies of knowledge and experience, especially in today's classrooms, what is read often elicits multiple interpretations, so reading achievement depends on the quality of the evidence students marshal in defense of their own interpretations.

With either definition, learning to read fluently requires sustained attention to printed material, but what kinds of attention? The logic of each definition leads to an opposite conclusion about how to engage the learner so she or he will focus the necessary time and sheer mindfulness to the task:

B1 Talking and Listening   (LR Handbook for Teachers K-6, Part B1)

Please comment on the child's development and use of spoken language in different social and curriculum contexts, in English and/or other languages: evidence of talk for learning and thinking; range and variety of talk for particular purposes; experience and confidence in talking and listening with different people in different settings.

A. was in my room last year, and an I.E.P. was established regarding his language processing. There has been much emphasis this year and last summer on language development, language experience, and verbalizing A.'s thoughts. It is evident from A.'s willingness to converse with me, shout out his discoveries, and to be able to respond to prompts when writing, that there is progress being made. He has responded well to read alouds, and is eager to volunteer his thoughts and predictions.   Sp.& Lang. has worked with A. in this area and indicates, "A. has shown a great deal of growth in his oral language skills this year. he is able to answer a variety of questions quickly, and appropriately, ask questins to peers and adults, and has been working on expanding his vocabulary skills through classification and categorizational activities. He interacts well with both peers and adults and participates in all the language activities presented to him." In class I have use many of the same prompts and techniques, and A. has continued to improve, gain confidence in speaking and feels confident in verbalizing his knowledge (2-26-97). He has improved his memorization skills and has recited poetry (1-27-97) to the class. Having A. last year and this year, has been rewarding as I have seen him go from reluctance & shrugging of shoulders to participation and excitement over class activities.

What experiences and teaching have helped/would help development in this area? Record outcomes of any discussions with other staff or parent(s).

It is of most importance that   RST &   Sp. & Lan.) confer again with Mom to give a supporting plan for summer months to carry over until the Fall. A. appears to need continued stimuli in language development activities to retain his acquired knowledge and to expand his development. At this time, A. still qualifies for the program, and it will be recommended that he continue in the Fall. Recommendation of less TV and more interacting activities ie, discussion, experiences & then retelling, actual hands on, sports have a definite positive affect on A.'s talking and listening skills.

FIGURE 2–17   Grade Three, boy. Language: English

■ The first envisions whole-class, teacher-led learning of a hierarchy of phonics "skills" in primary grades, with emphasis on the visual recognition of words and parts of words. Throughout the grade levels, reading in school means reading grade-leveled, vocabulary-controlled textbooks from which to derive established interpretations.

■ The second enlists readers at all levels in using their prior knowledge, interests, and experiences to learn to apply, with teacher help, a wide range of reading strategies—graphophonic, visual, syntactic, and context cues—to draw meaning from a broad array of literary and informational texts on intellectually and personally stimulating subjects.

Evidence of Progress Depends on Your Definition

In assessing student progress, the teacher who uses Definition 1 will most likely look for evidence that children can quickly recall specified sounds in isolation or within words, can pronounce nonsense words created to test knowledge of letter sounds, or can pronounce words without understanding what they mean. Opportunities to learn to read in this teacher's classroom will emphasize the memorization of letter sounds for immediate and automatic response to their appearance in print. Children will copy letters, words, and sentences in order to practice letter shapes and names and "sound out" words they do not know. The sequence of learning these sounds will probably proceed from sounds and letters in isolation to vocabulary-controlled stories—that is, those with words based on the phonics lessons already presented. Once children have learned to read aloud accurately, they begin to read in grade-level textbooks, answering questions designed to test their comprehension.

A teacher who, on the other hand, subscribes to Definition 2, looks for evidence that children are, first of all, using their own experience to find out what is revealed in printed materials of all kinds—stories in and outside of school, letters to and from real people, reports of information from newspapers, signs on buildings, comic books, and classics. Second, the teacher seeks proof that children are learning to use a range of reading strategies as well as their own backgrounds to make text comprehensible—for example, the sounds the letters within the words and together make, the pictures accompanying the text, the format and context of the content, the aspects of the reading that relate to the reader's experience. Opportunities to learn to read—activities and materials necessary to each child's developing literacy—result from the teacher's systematic observations of each child in different reading situations. Children demonstrate they can read trade books and each other's writing, newspapers, and labels, among an increasingly wide variety of other genre.

So which is the preferred definition of reading and what does it mean for assessing reading progress? Norm-referenced multiple-choice tests, reading workbooks, and grade-level reader tests? Journals, oral interpretations of text, portfolios of work, and multiple kinds of measures and learning situations? It all depends. Using the Learning Record to observe children closely as they learn to read and continue to read widely and deeply is strongly supportive of Definition 2. While this definition doesn't make teaching children to read easy, it does make it possible for teachers to integrate learning and assessment in a responsible way.

The Five Dimensions Can Help Teachers Document Reading Behaviors that Matter

The five dimensions of the learning continuum, as they are described on page 3, provide a framework for understanding the reading development of individual children, just as they do for learning stages in other areas of the curriculum. The dimensions of confidence and independence, experience, strategies, knowledge and understanding, as well as the ability to reflect provide the facets of the prism through which teachers observe student readers. Teachers use these dimensions to write about student progress, as it is reflected in their reading behaviors, in Part B2 of the Learning Record.

Because reading is language, it is learned like the other modes of language—talking, listening, and writing—through use for significant and authentic purposes. Learning to read and then learning to read all kinds of text are fundamentally important abilities for success in school. The LR, in recognition of these facts, provides two reading scales to measure development at the elementary levels. They are included as Appendix A. Revisiting the reading scales at several times during the year will help teachers stay focused on the types of observations and samples that need to be collected in order to make accurate scale placements.

Examples of B2

The samples shown in this section demonstrate how teachers collected observation notes and samples throughout the school year and made summary judgments of the students' reading progress through analysis of samples of student work toward the *end* of the third quarter. Teachers at that time also identified the stage of reading development reached by using the appropriate reading scale. Reading Scale 1 is used for Grades K–3; Scale 2 is used for Grades 4–8.

Mindy, whose record is shown as Figure 2–18, is a third grader who had demonstrated during the year that she is an "exceptionally fluent reader." Her teacher used Reading Scale 1 and her observations and samples of Mindy's work to arrive at this judgment. Quincy, Figure 2–19, is a fourth grader who is becoming a very competent reader. The teacher, who used Reading Scale 2 to determine his level as a "moderately experienced reader," summarized her observation and samples of his reading to back up this scale placement. Note how each teacher has summarized information from the Data Collection Form about what the students have read, how they have responded to it, and what this data shows they need next. Teachers observed their students in many different social and learning contexts: with known

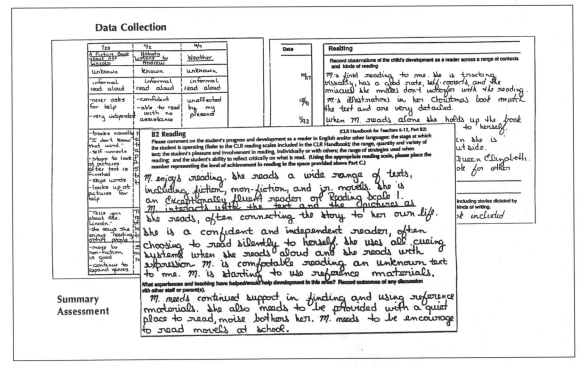

FIGURE 2–18 Grade Three, girl. Language: English

Grade Four, boy Languages: English	

Data Collection: Sampling

Dates	10-23-91
Title or book/text (literary or information)	The True Story of the Three Little Pigs
Known/unknown text	unknown
Sampling procedure used: informal assessment/running record/miscue analysis	informal
Overall impression of the child's reading: • confidence and degree of independence • involvement in the book/ text • the way in which the child reads the text aloud	very confident w/ text read w/expression + different voices for char.
Strategies the child used when reading aloud: • drawing on previous experience to make sense of the book/text • playing at reading • using book language • reading the pictures • focusing on print (directionality, 1:1 correspondence, recognition of certain words) • using semantic/syntactic/grapho-phonic cues • predicting • self-correcting • using several strategies or over-dependent on one	• related to known text of 3 Little Pigs • predicted what would happen next • self corrected - used context cues to figure out unknown words.
Child's response to the book/text: • personal response • critical response (understanding, evaluating, appreciating wider meanings)	• laughed at text and appreciated different point of view
What this sample shows about the child's development as a reader.	Moderately experienced reader
Experiences/support needed to further development.	need to direct to non-fiction books also

Data Collection:
Observation Notes

11-91	Q read _Ashanti to Zulu_ and _Ah, Mosquitoes Buzz in People's Ears_ to his Kinder-buddy. Q selected these books. He read fluently and with expression.
12-91	Q led his group in the performance of _Rumplestiltskin_. He helped his peers with unfamiliar words and explained his "trick" of "reading around the word" to a classmate.
2-92	Q chose books at the library that gave Science Fair ideas. He read them during SSR time.
2-92	Q created 5 commercials for his favorite "scary" books and shared them orally with the class.
3-92	Q collected poetry (mostly Silverstein) and made a book to read to his Kinder-Buddy.
4-92	Q read a different book each day after ASAT testing. (silently)

Summary Assessment

Q is a moderately experienced reader on Reading Scale 2. He likes reading fantasy and folktales. Q reads silently on a daily basis and often chooses reading as a form of recreation. As a "Kinder-Buddy," Q has read many books to his young friend. He has also created books or anthologies. Q uses context cues as his major cueing system. He tends to reflect by relating literature to personal experiences or other pieces of literature.

What learning experiences have helped/would help development in this area?

Q has begun to show interest in the area of science. More nonfiction/information books should be made available to him. The use of many references to write a report would be helpful to _____.

FIGURE 2–19   Grade Four, boy. Language: English

and unknown texts, in group and individual activities, in their responses to literature.

Teachers use the evidence of reading development in their observation notes together with student work samples as the bases for comments in Section B2 of the record. Figure 2–20 summarizes the reading progress of a fourth-grade girl whose mother described her at the beginning of the year as a reluctant reader. Described as an "inexperienced reader" on Reading Scale 2, Callie has engaged in a variety of learning experiences to increase her confidence as a reader. The teacher has introduced her to many different strategies for reading unfamiliar text in order to diminish Callie's reliance on the single strategy of decoding.

Although Callie, like Quincy, is a fourth grader, her book choices and the particulars of her responses to these books are those of a much less mature reader. Her teacher, like Quincy's, recognizes her struggle and supports her growing independence as a reader by (1) helping her use strategies to open up challenging texts, and (2) providing her with books to enjoy so she'll persevere with learning to read.

Writing

The Learning Record helps teachers continue (or begin) practices that support student use of writing as a process of thinking as well as a product for communicating. It will support them as they encourage students to write in many genres for many purposes and to use writing to learn subject matter content. Using the five dimensions of the learning continuum, they will be able to articulate specifically to students and their parents what students' writing strengths are and what students need in the way of experiences to develop those strengths even further.

Two Definitions of Writing

To assess and promote the progress children make in their abilities to express themselves in writing, parents and teachers must consider how they define writing. Is writing defined as *transcription* (the lettering of regularly spelled and conventionally formatted words on a page or computer screen) or *composition* (the creation and arrangement of text to convey meaning)? Or as a combination of both?

B2 Reading (CLR Handbook for Teachers K-6, Part B2)

Please comment on the child's progress and development as a reader in English and/or other languages: the stage at which the child is operating (refer to the reading scales, Appendix A); the range, quantity and variety of reading in all areas of the curriculum; the child's pleasure and involvement in story and reading, alone or with others; the range of strategies used when reading and the child's ability to reflect critically on what is read. (Using the appropriate reading scale, please place the number representing the level of achievement in reading in the space provided above Part C.)

Ca___ has struggled off and on throughout the year but has shown that with motivation and a variety of tasks that take her "into, thru, and beyond" a piece of text she is very successful. Her focus for tackling difficult text was to sound out a difficult word. Throughout the year she was able to gain comprehension from reading in context, drawing pictures from text, acting out scenes from the stories and predicting, questioning, commenting thoughts. Ca___'s statement at the beginning of the year "I don't like to read" has been changed to "Reading is O.K." Her involvement in several books indicates that she likes reading.

What experiences and teaching have helped/would help development in this area? Record outcomes of any discussion with other staff or parent(s).

Provide a variety of texts in many different genre with reading levels that are challenging, easy and in-between. Continue to provide Ca___ with strategies that can help her when she's reading alone (ex: using context, pictures, etc.)

FIGURE 2–20   Grade Four, girl. Language: English

If the definition of writing focuses solely or primarily on transcription, instruction and assessment will be concerned with the appearance of the child's text—for example, the formation of letters, spelling, punctuation, and paragraphing. The purpose of the teaching of writing and its assessment, using this definition, is to help students become scribes who can physically write down text accurately—that is, without error. Because correctness of form takes precedence over the child's development of recognition of conventions, early writing may stress copying from the texts of others or dictating to adults who will write the words correctly. Later, children may finish sentence or essay prompts, such as "My favorite holiday is . . ." Assessment of progress in writing, using this definition, involves analysis of what is written in terms of adherence to set rules for accuracy in writing on given topics in specified forms.

If the definition of writing is one concerned with composition, what is expressed takes on primary importance, with transcription elements seen as a means to making the writing clear to others. Teachers assessing progress with this goal in mind provide a variety of writing situations so children can learn to adapt what they want to say to meet the needs of a variety of readers for all the different purposes people have for writing. It is obvious that students who read widely and well become familiar with well-crafted models of writing for many different purposes. For this reason, reading and writing must be taught as complements to each other.

To assess writing achievement, then, parents, teachers, and students themselves must consider both definitions—composition and transcription—together, rather than separately. The primary focus, however, should be placed on substance, clarity, and style as elements of writing well. Transcription is inseparable from these composing elements and should not be isolated in assessment. Student writers must not only learn to address effectively what their readers need to know about their topic, but they must also show they are increasingly able to use conventions—such as preferred spellings, reader-friendly punctuation, and content-appropriate paragraphing—to permit their readers full and easy access to their ideas. In addition, assessments of writing should promote the notion that students use resources such as dictionaries, style books, and human respondents as they write, for the same reasons adult writers use them.

The Five Dimensions Also Help Teachers Document Writing

Teachers who use the LR provide a wide range of learning situations in their classrooms to ensure engagement by all students, and they know their students well enough to know the kinds of opportunities each needs in order to learn. One fourth-grade teacher described the goal of observing children, the benefits, and the rigor required to know learners. "I want to be able not only to observe but to come to some conclusions about what I've observed—I should know what it all means after I've observed. I feel this process is opening up a new avenue for me as a teacher to see the 'whole' child—not

simply a statistic or rather a child at 'such and such' a level. . . . To observe, really observe, nonjudgmentally, it takes practice, care, and patience."

Teachers who use the LR extend their understandings of what students are learning. Teachers use the learning dimensions to ask specifically, "What can my observation notes and writing samples tell me about what my students know and what they are learning to do?" Below are the notes she made of her observations of Joyce as the first grader wrote a story. Her observations describe the child's writing process and the context for the writing. A writing sample, Figure 2–21, shows the product.

Joyce told her story aloud continually while writing and drawing. She did no revision at first and seemed to jump around in her thinking. In rereading her story, however, she recognized that the word *from* was spelled correctly and was excited to share this discovery. She used invented spelling: *stru* for *sister* and *frund* for *friend*. She revised spelling of *friends* by squeezing an *n* in the right place. She orally sounded out the words when spelling them. She used a period after *my* in *my mom*. She responded to her writing by saying that she was writing about

FIGURE 2–21   Grade One, girl. Language: English

her sister because she loves her sister. Her audience was her mom. Joyce orally told a story with a beginning, middle, and end. When discussing the sentence "We were separated," she went back to add "at school," and then drew a picture to go with it. Her illustration shows Joyce at school raising her hand to answer a question.

Confidence and Independence

2/7 J. worked throughout writer's workshop, writing and drawing for about 20 minutes. She used invented spelling without over concern for perfection.

2/15 J. chose her topic for writing with eagerness. She drew a picture of herself opening a present from her mom; then she went back and included her twin sister.

Experience

2/15 J.'s story about her mom and sister is one of a series of pictures and stories about her family. She writes about things that happen at home and sometimes at school. Love, friendship, and family are her themes at this point in her writing.

Strategies

2/7 J. used both beginning and ending sounds of words to help her spell unfamiliar words when writing.

2/15 J. tells the story aloud as she is writing it. Her oral story is much more elaborate than the one she writes down. She draws the pictures first and then does the writing around the pictures.

2/15 J. uses invented spelling: *stru* for *sister* and *frund* for *friend*. She orally sounded out the words as she spelled them.

Knowledge and Understanding

2/13 J. read a story in writer's chair from a book she was working on that at that point only had blank pages. She made

up an elaborate story with a plot sequence and details. She would pause and tell the audience, "This is the fun part." She paused several times, looked at the audience of children, tutors, and teachers, and made positive comments about their good listening behavior.

Reflectiveness

2/15 J. said that she was writing this story about her sister because she loves her sister. She wants her mom to read the story. She sees her writing as a way of making and maintaining connections with people she loves and casting things in a positive light. She did a picture showing her at school raising her hand to answer a question.

Examples of B3

Over a period of five months Hilary has demonstrated impressive development as a writer, as shown in Figure 2–22. At the beginning of the year, her teacher noted her confidence as she shared her writing in the "author's chair." Throughout the year, Hilary's teacher documented her growing skill and use of strategies to tackle the problems she met as she wrote. She also observed her in many different social settings. Hilary's confidence, observed across a range of situations, demonstrates her independence as a writer. The teacher's notes also reveal much about the classroom opportunities to read and write alone and in large- and small-group settings. Hilary obviously enjoys many resources and authentic situations to help her as she learns to write for many purposes and readers.

In this account of the progress Ben has made in becoming a writer (Figure 2–23), the teacher summarizes her observation notes and her analyses of the three writing samples collected throughout the year. She describes specifically the gains he has made, within the framework of the five dimensions of learning as they apply to becoming a writer: a growth in confidence and indepen-

Writing

Record observations of the child's development as a writer (including stories dictated by the child when appropriate) across a range of contexts and kinds of writing.

10'96	Guided writing with teacher during writing workshop. H. asks for help to write the word tower. T. asks her to say it slowly, H. then writes TR for tower. Shares her picture in the author's chair and says, "This is my tower and I colored it with rainbow tiles."
10'96	During large group interactive writing, H. said that the word FLOOR ended with R< came and wrote the letter on the overhead, wrote a lower case r. During writing workshop H. drew a picture of Pocohontas, and wrote POC. Shared it in the author's chair, and said, "this is my Pocohontas doll because I have the movie."
11'96	Free choice time - H. writes letters to friends, takes out and copies name cards, sometimes reads name cards. Writes TO___ on outside of envelope, and FROM on inside card, then puts letters in the mailbox.
12'96	Working alone during writing workshop. Wrote: "Im at the pk w JJodi." Read the words back to teacher, used dictionary for the words the, at, sounded out other words. Left spaces between almost all the words, wrote left to right, and had return sweep.
1-97	H. is the mailcarrier, and reads and matches names to names of lockers and delivers mail.
2'97	During large group writing H. says the word SISTERS has an R in it, comes and writes lower case r in word.

FIGURE 2–22 Grade Kindergarten, girl. Language: English

B3 Writing   (CLR Handbook, Part B3)

Please comment on the child's progress and development as a writer in English and/or other languages: the degree of confidence and independence as a writer; the range, quantity and variety of writing in all areas of curriculum; the child's pleasure and involvement in writing both narrative and non-narrative, alone and in collaboration with others; the influence of reading on the child's writing; growing understanding of written language, its conventions and spelling.

B. has made much progress with his writing this year, and he is now becoming a confident writer. At the beginning of the year he wrote as little as possible, and was very bothered by misspellings. His last piece of writing this year was a collaboration between him and Dustin. They conferenced about the problem that the story was to have and then they each chose a part to write on their own. He is now willing to

What experiences and teaching have helped/would help development in this area? Record outcomes of any discussion with other staff or parent(s). make "guesses" when he is spelling. He uses common punctuation marks rather consistently and is aware of other punctuation. B's increased book knowledge is showing up in the things he chooses to write about eg. Flintstones.

B. needs to continue to be encouraged not to worry about perfection in an initial draft. Having someone write for him when time is a factor can be helpful.

Signed: Class Teacher_____ Date:_____

Other Staff Contributor(s)_____ Date:_____

FIGURE 2–23 Grade Three, boy. Language: English

dence; his ability to use his prior experience; his ability to apply his developing writing skills and strategies; his ability to draw on his knowledge from course content; and his reflectiveness about his own writing capabilities.

Ben at this time exhibits confidence as a writer. Earlier in the year, he had resisted writing, insisting on correctness in first drafts. Now, he gets his thoughts down, using approximate spellings, which can be dealt with when he edits. He has demonstrated that he can apply learning strategies such as (1) collaborating with a partner to generate ideas about both content and form and (2) reading more to expand the possible topics to write about. He has also demonstrated that he is learning to apply punctuation conventions to what he writes. In addition to describing what Ben has shown he has learned, the teacher also recommends next steps to learning more, so that Ben's parents, next year's teacher, and Ben himself can build on this year's accomplishments.

English Language Learners

In Figure 2–24, a fourth-grade girl, newly arrived from Hong Kong, writes a story about Rumpelstiltskin. In this writing sample, she demonstrates writing fluency. Even though her teacher knew no Chinese, she learned from the girl's oral language in class that she was obviously acquiring English as a second language, and this sample shows she is doing it without losing her primary means of expressing and developing her ideas. See Appendix B for the Stages of English Lanquage Learning.

A fourth-grade girl who has only been in the United States a year and a half writes in her native tongue, Spanish, Figure 2–25. The teacher translates the story into English to share with others in the class who do not know Spanish. This exchange is of benefit to English-only speakers as well as to the girl learning English. The more all children understand that knowing more than one language is an advantage, not a deficit, the better equipped they will be to communicate broadly with respect for difference.

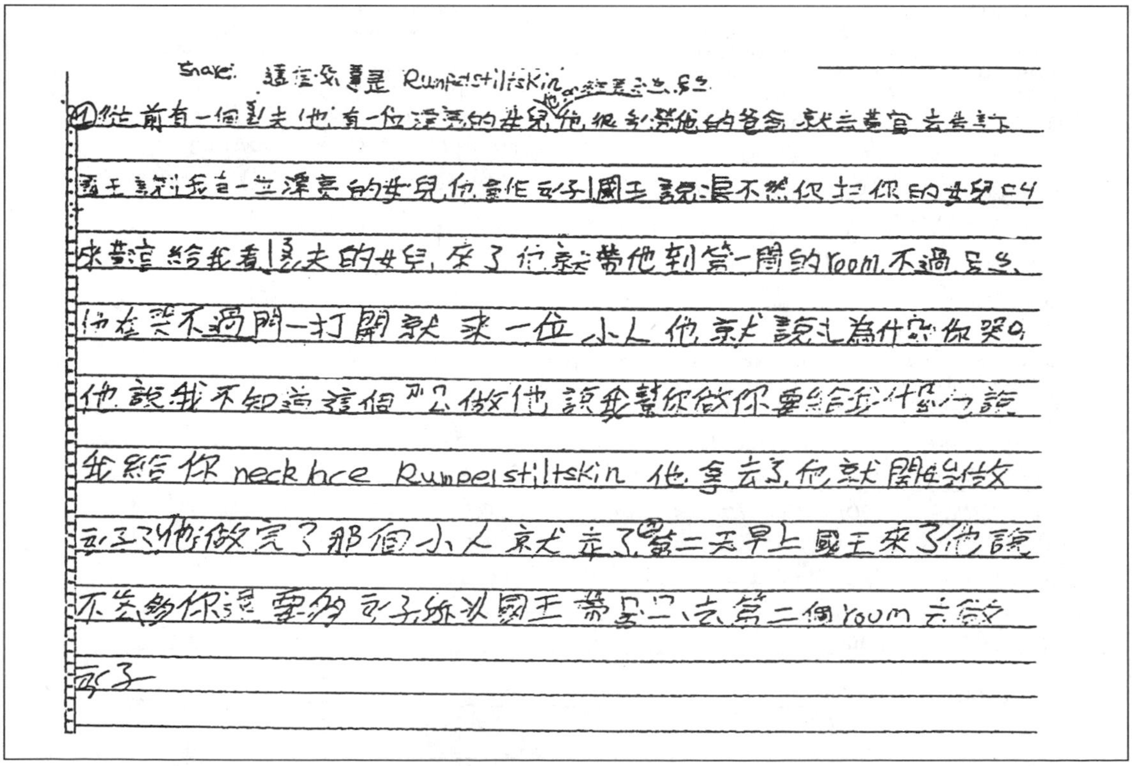

FIGURE 2–24 Grade Four, girl. Languages: Chinese, English

A Via una ves un gato que es tava
Once upon a time there was a cat, that was

muerta y un difunta y es pantavan a las noche
dead and a ghost.   In the night they scared

a las personas y las personas que vian
people.   When the people saw the dead

el gato x el difunto que estavan muertos
cat and ghost they were always scared.

y se es pantavan las personas cuando

los vian y asta se desmallavan las
                The people fainted and then the dead

personas y luego se i sieron buenos
and the ghost became good dead people.

y las quisieron a los difuntos

i ese es mi cuenta
And this is my story.

FIGURE 2–25   Grade Four, girl. Languages: Spanish, English

Although the Learning Record is designed for use as children enter school, a deaf preschool boy's record illustrates the use of the LR to acknowledge American Sign Language (ASL) as a primary language that serves as the basis for the child's learning English as a second language. In Figure 2–26, a university researcher's reading samples, collected on one day, show the extent of his emerging literacy. The samples plus her observations, not shown, are summarized in Figure 2–27.

The LR places a value on a student's home literacies and community languages because it not only ensures that families can continue to support their children's schooling as they add English to their primary language, but it also enhances their learning. The primary language represents much of the child's prior experience on which he or she must build literacy. As children learn to use English, they should be encouraged to speak and write in the "nearest-at-hand" language in order to develop their ideas more fully without the impediment of translating. As they become fluent in English,

3 Reading Samples (Reading in English and/or other languages) To include reading aloud and reading silently			(CLR Handbook for teachers K-6, Part B)
Dates	5/98	5/98	5/98
Title or book/text (literary or information)	The Very Hungry Caterpillar	Bears in the Night	Downey & Buttercup
Known/unknown text	known	known	known
Sampling procedure used: informal assessment/ running record/ miscue analysis	informal/videotape	informal/videotape	informal/videotape
Overall impression of the child's reading: • confidence and degree of independence • involvement in the book/text • the way in which the child reads the text aloud	confident and very engaged	confident and very engaged	not as confident, but retold from the picture
Strategies used when reading aloud: • drawing on previous experience to make sense of the book/text ■ playing at reading • using book language • reading the pictures • focusing on print (directionality, 1:1 correspondence, recognition of certain words) • using semantic, syntactic and graphophonic cues • predicting • self-correcting • using several strategies or over-dependence on one	Not focused on the print of the book, but follows the action of the story as depicted in the pictures. Signs on the page to help explain the actions of caterpillar. Becomes the caterpillar and "munches" each piece of fruit/candy on the pages sequentially. Indicates with appropriate signs and facial expressions the sick feeling of the caterpillar after eating all the food. Signs and approximates English for butterfly	Turns each page and signs the action depicted on the page. Ask if the road is for a train-uses vehicle sign to follow the path of the road. Uses classifers to indicate the bears walking, running or jumping through the forest, falling down the hill and jumping into bed.	Turns each page and tells the story by following the action depicted on the page. Signs on the page as in previous samples. Uses body language, gestures and facial expressions to depict the different characters in the story.
Child's response to the book/text: • personal response • critical response (understanding, evaluating, appreciating wider meanings	Clearly understands that the story has a beginning, middle and end. Enjoys becoming the caterpillar and munching all the food until he is very fat and sick	Enjoys the action filled story of the bears going through the forest. Has a clear understanding of the story through the pictures. Renactment is picture governed	Enjoyed the story even though his renactment was not as clear as the other two samples.
What this sample shows about the child's development as a reader.	Becoming a reader. Understands that books have stories and each page contributes to the overall story.	Becoming a reader. Understands that books have stories and each page contributes to the overall story.	Becoming a reader. Understands that books have stories and each page contributes to the overall story.
Experience/support needed to further development.	Roleplay stories and encourage elaboration	Roleplay stories and encourage elaboration	Roleplay stories and encourage elaboration

* Early indicators that the child is moving into reading   Please attach text samples described on this sheet.

Published as a component of The Learning Record Assessment System. For further information, call or write the Center for Language in Learning at 10610 Quail Canyon Road, El Cajon, CA 92021 (619) 443-6320. Computer application created by Intelligent Solutions. © 1995 by Saul Kitmaly.

FIGURE 2–26   Grade Pre-Kindergarten, boy.
Languages: ASL, English

B2 Reading

(CLR Handbook for Teachers K-6, Part B2)

Please comment in your own words on the child's progress and development as a reader in English and/or other languages: the stage at which the child is operating; the range, quantity and variety of reading in all areas of the curriculum; the child's pleasure and involvement in story and reading, alone or with others; the range of strategies used when reading and the child's ability to reflect critically on what is read. **Refer to the appropriate reading scale.**

D   is "Becoming A Reader" (Reading Scale 1). The daily exposure to books and printed texts has facilitated his understanding that books have interesting information and stories are meaningful. He understands that there is a development of a story and uses the pictures to re-enact or retell the story alone and with others (picture-governed). He is also aware of print and that it carries information specifically, the connection that there is a 1 to 1 correspondence between the handshapes of fingerspelling and letter printed on a page as well as the letters he can print. This has been demonstrated when he fingerspells his name, the names of his classmates and characters in books. After the story is presented by the teachers in ASL and English, D   has been observed most often with an adult retelling the story or waiting for the adult to tell him the story again. He turns each page very carefully demonstrating further his understanding that books and stories have a beginning, middle and end. He appears to enjoy stories that are dynamic and action packed. This was demonstrated when he was asked to choose a book to read to the evaluator. He also showed the most interest with these kinds of stories during story time.

He was observed during storytime and booksharing for the following books-Don't Cut My Hair, McDuff, Peter Rabbit, and The Three Billy Goats Gruff.

What experiences and teaching have helped/would help development in this area? Record outcomes of any discussions with other staff or parent(s).

D   needs continued exposure to a variety of books as well as repetition of stories to further develop his comprehension of the stories in ASL and English. Connections between the printed word and ASL need to be highlighted in order to foster his literacy development in both languages e.g. dictated stories to teachers and adults, word walls, and class books. The student centered environment, thematic & integrated activities, booksharing sessions should also continue. Exposure to ASL stories such as number stories, ABC stories would foster his ASL literacy. A team approach to storytelling has facilitated his metalinguistic awareness of ASL and English as well as his social interactions with bilingual children and adults, hearing and deaf and should continue.

FIGURE 2–27   Grade Pre-Kindergarten, boy. Languages: ASL, English

they will make the switch to using it for generating and shaping their ideas, too, especially as they share their work with fluent English speakers.

The *Primary Language Record Handbook for Teachers* explains it this way:

Bilingual children may well be developing as readers and writers in their first languages and, given the opportunity, can use this developing competence in the mainstream classroom. The child writing partly in one language and partly in the other is one obvious possibility, but some children may also wish to write at length in their first language, without necessarily recasting the writing into English. This kind of activity is valuable in itself, but is also useful as a way of increasing a child's awareness of the similarities and differences between different language systems. Thought needs to be given to the fact that children

writing in community languages will need some response to their writing, and the possibility of sharing it with an audience.

It is important that children feel that their first language is valued in the classroom and that they can make choices about the language they write in.

When recording bilingual children's progress in writing in English, it will be important to note the length of time they have been learning English.

The LR supports teachers as they encourage students to use their primary language as well as acquire a second language. Bilingualism is considered an acccomplishment valuable enough to be shared and incorporated into the assessment system. The English language itself remains the common language of education, with second languages perceived as a benefit to all.

Reflecting on the Year's Work

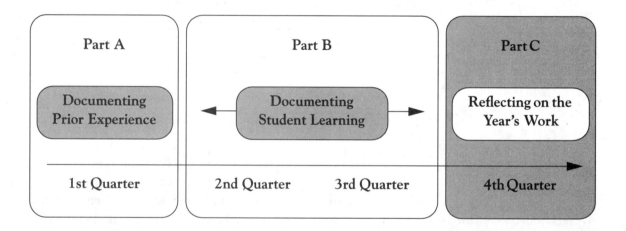

In Part C, parents and students reflect upon the record of achievement described in Parts A and B and add further comments to complete the year's picture of the student's development. The teacher updates the record and recommends the next steps to be taken.

Parents contribute to Part C1 of the LR after they review their child's record of achievement for the year. Typically, they voice a new perspective of the child as a learner, of the school as supportive of their family goals, and of themselves as collaborative educators.

Parents are generally enthusiastic about the Learning Record. "This narrative report," one parent told the teacher, "is an excellent strategy for the student because teachers, students, and parents can clearly see the development of the student from the start up to the end of the school year. It motivates parents to assist their son or daughter, and helps me picture the activities and development of my son and set goals for him at home."

In C2, the students reflect upon Parts A and B and add further comments to complete the year's picture of their development. In C3, the present teacher provides updated information for next year's teacher to use.

Jerry's teacher, in Figure 3–1, held the C1 and C2 conferences at the same time so Jerry could hear what his father had to say about his scholastic achievement. The

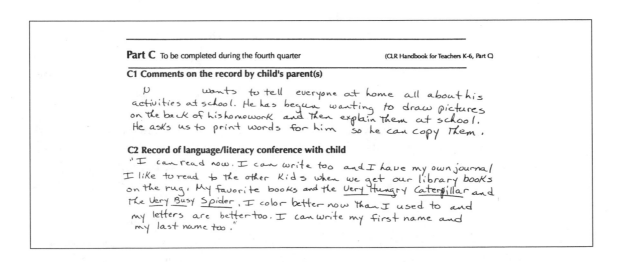

Part C To be completed during the fourth quarter

C1 Comments on the record by child's parent(s)

I really enjoyed reading this report because it gave me an opportunity to sort of be in the classroom and experience what J____ does in class. I couldn't get that from a report card. It's almost like a Nova event, in which you have grades for each aspect of your performance, but until you actually read the write-up, it doesn't really tell you a lot.

C2 Record of language/literacy conference with child

I was present as I conferenced with his father. He commented that he liked writing his story of "Jack & the Beans Stew" and having it published for the class book. He is proud of the fact that he had his own collection of books at home to use and enjoy.

C3 Information for receiving teacher
This section is to ensure that information for the receiving teacher is as up to date as possible. Please comment on changes and development in any aspect of the child's learning since Part B was completed.

J____ has developed his fluency in writing this year and has had the opportunity to be exposed to a variety of literary genres. He has moved confidently along the continuum of Reading Scale 2 to become a moderately experienced reader who can handle a variety of genres.

What experiences and teaching have helped/would help development? Record outcomes of any discussion with other staff, or parent(s).

I would encourage J____ to be exposed to an ever greater variety of authors. He is at a point in his reading development where he would benefit from exposure to additional ways to use a library for research and to continue to broaden his experience.

Signed: Parent(s) _____ Date: 5/22/92

Class Teacher _____ Date: 5/22/92

Other Staff Contributor(s) _____ Date: _____

FIGURE 3–1   Grade Three, boy. Languages: Tagalog, English

teacher quoted the father directly and paraphrased Jerry's comments. Ned's father, in Figure 3–2, explains his son's excitement over school activities and in the process reveals how he is supporting his son's learning. Ned himself, after examining his portfolio and his record, reflects on how much he has learned over the course of a year.

The parent's comments for Brenda, a fifth grader, in Figure 3–3, provide another illustration of specific ways the teacher recognizes officially on the record how the home supports

Part C To be completed during the fourth quarter   (CLR Handbook for Teachers K-6, Part C)

C1 Comments on the record by child's parent(s)

N____ wants to tell everyone at home all about his activities at school. He has begun wanting to draw pictures on the back of his homework and then explain them at school. He asks us to print words for him so he can copy them.

C2 Record of language/literacy conference with child

"I can read now. I can write too and I have my own journal I like to read to the other kids when we get our library books on the rug. My favorite books and the Very Hungry Caterpillar and the Very Busy Spider. I color better now than I used to and my letters are better too. I can write my first name and my last name too."

FIGURE 3–2   Grade Kindergarten, boy. Language: English

Part C To be completed during the fourth quarter (CLR Handbook for Teachers K-6, Part C)

C1 Comments on the record by child's parent(s) *See letter attached!* (Copied fr. Parent Letter)

B has had a fantastic year. She has grown with amazing speed. Not only physically but her mentality has grown as well. Her reading ability has soared. She now understands what she reads and can answer questions about the story.

Her math ability has grown. She has done wonderful this year. She has grown beyond my hopes. Thank you Mrs. for the wonderful job this year.

Thanks. —m

C2 Record of language/literacy conference with child You have done with B

See attached writing from child.

B feels very successful and mature about her year. She is starting to read the same books her mom reads. This is a far cry from Dr. Seuss and Amelia Bedelia in September. Her New Year's goal was to improve herself as a student. She certainly has done that. She says she loves to read. She says her older sisters treats her with more respect now that she is smarter and acts better.

FIGURE 3–3   Grade Five, girl. Language: English

classroom instruction. Such a connection needs to be built if the child is to extend on the considerable experience she brings to school.

In Figure 3–4, a second-grade boy's comments are written as he dictated them to his teacher—in Spanish. He reveals that he is becoming very conscious of his own power as a learner. The teacher uses direct and indirect quotes to summarize the parent's comments at a conference near the end of the year.

In Figure 3–5, Vivian, a second-grade girl, and her parent reflect upon her year as a

C1 Comments on the record by child's parent(s)

H. está leyendo muchísimo en casa, y aunque todavía le cuesta no abandona su lucha. Ya nos tiene a todos aburridos de tanto leernos y hablarnos". También está escribiendo mejor, aunque allí "todavía le vemos muchos problemas porque se brinca letras". "Pero qué le digo, ha mejorado tanto que no lo podemos creer. Ahora hasta escribe cartas a sus tíos de Tijuana." "Todos le tenemos paciencia porque vemos que él sabe muchas cosas pero le cuesta escribirlos

C2 Record of language/literacy conference with child

"Ahora ya la hice, ya no me aburro tanto, maestri. Ahora ya soy un autor, porque ya escribo mis propios cuentos. Lo que me pasa es que nunca las termino". Le pregunté por qué y su respuesta fue "para que los que lo leen se queden con las ganas, mejor que ellos le inventen el final, ¿para qué voy a ponerle final si Ud. después nos dice: 'a ver niños y niñas, ahora Uds. le van a poner un final diferente"!

FIGURE 3–4   Grade Two, boy. Languages: Spanish, English

Part C To be completed during the fourth quarter (CLR Handbook, Part C)

C1 Comments on the record by child's parent(s)

V has made significant progress this year. Her confidence level has increased. V loves writing at home. She rarely asks for help in spelling and would rather do it on her own and try and sound the words out. She still has a tendency to stick to familar things. She tends to mix up her B's, D's, and P's. She also seems to want to write her numbers - six and nines backwords. With two older sister's close to her own age and trying to be her teacher, she enjoy's the chance to help and teach someone else. She enjoy's reading to herself. Each evening we try to set aside time for her to read aloud to mom or dad. She still needs more confidence and is a bit shy. She has improved in all areas thru the year. She enjoys school and looks forward to going every day.

C2 Record of language/literacy conference with child V says she enjoyed reading Smarty Pants this year" because it was easy. "She thinks she's a better reader and says that she likes to read with friends. She said the writing activity she liked the most was Journals; "because we just get to write what we want."

FIGURE 3–5   Grade Two, girl. Language: English

reader. Both share the child's favorite experiences and determine that she has made considerable progress, both at home and at school. Her parent expresses concern about reversals, and for the most part, views Vivian's progress at home as a complement to her progress at school.

The teacher, in Figure 3–6, describes in C3 the progress Jason has made during the year. She emphasizes the effect of encouragement on his commendable journey in becoming a reader. She also validates the home support Jason receives. The teacher reflects upon the student's achievements and highlights the student's greatest strengths upon which the receiving teacher can build new opportunities for further development.

The same teacher writes Part C for Ella, another child in her class the same year in Figure 3–7. The comments are different for each because the teacher knows well the strengths each has to build on and the next steps they must take in their personalized education.

Overall, Part C allows for fourth-quarter growth to be reported. It also encourages parents and the student to participate in recognizing and evaluating the year's work by the student. Most important, it endorses a view of learning as ongoing and cumulative. In Figure 3–8, the three stakeholders in Cindy's schooling—parent, child, and teacher—demonstrate the value of this update to her record of achievement at the end of fourth grade.

J has made considerable progress this year. In the area of reading he started out the year comfortable with only family texts which we had read together or that he had read in kindergarten. By the middle of the second quarter I determined that he was a "non-fluent reader" as described on the Reading scale 1. By June, he has become a confident fluent reader as described on the fourth level of the scale

What experiences and teaching have helped/would help development? Record outcomes of any discussion with other staff, or parent(s).

Constant encouragement and exposure to a wide range of reading materials at school has helped J. make strides in the development of his reading skills. His diligence and determination as a student cannot be minimized in contribution to this progress. He has also had considerable and consistent support at home in his development as a learner.

FIGURE 3–6 Grade One, boy. Languages: Tagalog, English

C Information for receiving teacher
This section is to ensure that information for the receiving teacher is as up to date as possible. Please comment on changes and development in any aspect of the child's learning since Part B was completed.

E. is a bright and enthusiastic learner, a student with exceptional listening skills and one who truly enjoys listening to stories aloud. When she tackles an unfamiliar book she looks mostly at the pictures to give her clues about how to read the words.

What experiences and teaching have helped/would help development? Record outcomes of any discussion with other staff, or parent(s).

E. has strong support at home with talk and listening and reading. She has already started her own collection of books and tapes which she knows by heart. As she learns new stories and songs, I would now encourage her to make regular connections between the words she speaks and the letters on the page. She already has a good foundation for this.

Signed: Parent(s) E.R. Date: 6/22/92
Class Teacher S. M. Date: 6/17/92
Other Staff Contributor(s) ______ Date: ______

FIGURE 3–7 Grade One, girl. Languages: Spanish, English

Part C To be completed during the fourth quarter

C1 Comments on the record by child's parent(s)
Mom feels that C progress in wanting to read has increased tremendously. "She sits down to read – there's no struggle." She also feels that her whole attitude toward school is very positive and relates this to the work in this class. Mom appreciates having the one to one contact with the teacher and feels that this communication helps in the success of her child's education.

C2 Record of language/literacy conference with child
C feels that her attitude towards reading has changed a little. The activities in class helped her to become more interested and helped her read faster and with better understanding. She felt that the journals were helpful because she could "flip back" to see if she forgot something or help her understanding of what she's reading. Writing has become more exciting and she feels she's improved her neatness.

C3 Information for receiving teacher
This section is to ensure that information for the receiving teacher is as up to date as possible. Please comment on changes and development in any aspect of the child's learning since Part B was completed.
C 's ability to take information previously learned and put it into the context of current learning is an asset. Her love for working with others can be fostered but she also thrives when finishing a project alone. Continued reading/writing connections can be made with lots of varied assignments.

What experiences and teaching have helped/would help development? Record outcomes of any discussion with other staff, or parent(s).
More practice with a writing process approach to writing, more one on one (child w/adult) learning situations, and more strategy instruction for readers tackling difficult text will help development

Signed: Parent(s) C Date: 5-20-93
Class Teacher M Date: 5-20-93
Other Staff Contributor(s) ______ Date: ______

FIGURE 3–8 Grade Four, girl. Language: English

Classroom Organization and Management

Students need teachers who know their students' full measure, the school reform literature tells us. It is, after all, teachers who must provide space, time, and occasion for their students to develop the knowledge and strategies they need to meet the academic standards set for them. Such a mandate requires that when students are not comprehending a task or performing well, teachers can assist each of them *directly* to understand concepts through questions, feedback, and the "scaffolding" of relevant experience. Teachers of elementary-aged children can set up enabling environments such as these only when they know those children well enough to show them useful reading strategies, introduce just the right book, provide the apt comment, arrange the most productive classroom exchanges, and enlist children in providing evidence of their own learning.

Classrooms Must Allow Teachers and Students to Share Responsibility for Assessment

In these favorable contexts, children can demonstrate, for themselves and others, that they are progressing toward desired goals.

Teachers determine just how competent each student is becoming by documenting what they observe students demonstrate orally or in writing in classroom activities, as they sort out their budding thoughts and open them up for sharing and for revising. With teacher and child sharing the goals and the criteria by which attainment is measured, both can focus on recognizing what students can do and working on what is next to be learned.

How can teachers create classrooms where children can learn to assess their own progress? How can they provide the kinds of strategic opportunities and feedback students need? How can they set up a structure so that children can collaborate in demonstrating what they know and can do? Can they provide activities which allow children to use age-appropriate criteria to determine the quality of their performance? Can they organize their classrooms so that children can assume responsibility for assessment?

Teachers Turn to Portfolios

Because of their involvement in the move to standards-referenced assessment and the consequent changes they and their students must make, teachers know, better than most, the effects of heavy reliance on single answer, on-demand tests to define academic achievement. Tests such as these assess some aspects of what most students know, but they fail to assess accurately and fully what individual students know. In the case of culturally and linguistically different students, these tests are especially inimical to both the fruits of personal experience and the opportunities to learn afforded at school.

The need to know about student progress, however, is an integral part of improving education. And, teachers, as the professionals closest to the student, have to lead the reform in assessment. Many have moved to student portfolios as a way to capture student growth over time as well as a way to involve students in the evaluation of their own work. The Learning Record fits in this movement in that it helps teachers manage assessment by portfolio. It answers the question that usually arises about what to do with student work once it is collected. And, further, it is an organization tool. As more than one teacher has remarked, "Organization is a weakness for me. Ways to keep track." The LR helps such teachers—as well as students and their parents—keep track, not only of their students' progress but also of the instruction they need to provide.

Questions Asked and Answered by Teachers

Teachers familiar with the LR were asked to answer five questions often asked by teachers and administrators about the various ways the LR works for them and the kinds of classroom practices it supports. Their answers to the questions below shed some light about solutions to commonly cited apprehensions, and they also hint at the changes they have made in their teaching. Probably, however, the most important aspect of their answers is their determination to find them. Convinced that the LR is simply good for children, the teachers described here developed strategies for changing their classrooms and adapting

their practices. Here are some questions they ask themselves regularly, and their answers.

Where do I find the time to have conferences and observe students during my regular school day?

First-Grade Teacher: You trade time. You don't have to give up any time. You give up old practices and replace them with different ones. Instead of grading papers, you get out your observation [tools].

Another First-Grade Teacher: More time does not need to be found because new priorities are made with the existing amount of time. Once the organization of the class is conducive to observations, then the actual observations become second nature with practice. Many teachers focus on three to four students a day. Others plan to observe only during a given time period. Teachers must have the mindset that observations are very important and must be complete to assure the best education to all students. Students should be active learners during the observation time, . . . working independently, in pairs, or small groups. Many teachers I know found it easy to begin observing during a time when all students are reading independently.

Third-Grade Teacher: Since I have come to consider this an essential part of my teaching, I have built observation into the schedule; the students know it and plan for it just as I do. They know this is a time when they have to be completely independent or work with a buddy. The time I plan into the schedule is during a language arts activity period.

Another Third-Grade Teacher: From the beginning I talk about independence and responsibility. I model reading and writing in the beginning so they see me as a reader and writer also. I talk about books I read and share my writing. I go sit at the different tables during writing and write my stories too. I have thousands of books in my room all the time, and we talk about books several times a day. I guess this is the modeling I use to help them become readers and writers. And when you read and write, times passes quickly. I don't need any [artificial] activities, seat work, or teacher-planned work. I do require that a log of reading be kept up to date and that responses to reading be done weekly. There are also expectations for writers' workshop.

Another Third-Grade Teacher: I conference with one to three children a day; however, there may be days when I don't have any conferences. I might be working on projects with students or doing observations for my anecdotal records.

What are the students doing while I observe?

Fifth-Grade Teacher: As I started to internalize the philosophy behind the LR, I realized that my place in the classroom had to change if I wanted more time to conference with individual students and to observe. So I read a lot, observed some colleagues, and asked a lot of questions. . . . Once I set up a structure for the students I was free to observe them at work.

Third-Grade Teacher: I may choose to conference during a Reading Workshop period when I can pull a student over to a table in the corner of my room for a teacher-student conference. This gives everyone the message that this is student conference time with the teacher and there should be no disturbances. Another time that works well is during Writing Workshop time when all the students are involved in some aspect of the writing process. This is especially a great time to observe if I am not in demand for participating in a writing response group. It definitely is part of the training process to establish this conferencing and observing as part of my routine to assist them with their learning. I think that it is important to communicate this to parents early in the year so they know that this will be a part of the class routine.

Another Third-Grade Teacher: I observe when my students are working independently, in pairs, or small groups. Many teachers found it easy to begin observing during a time when all students are reading independently.

Another Third-Grade Teacher: When I conference with one child, the other children are reading, responding in logs, or writing. They need long periods of time, too, to do their reading and writing. Students enjoy and appreciate these long uninterrupted times. I keep flexible and feel the mood of the day. If the students aren't settled into their reading and writing, I don't conference until I have the feeling that everyone is engaged. Students like conference time, so I think they respect that time when other students are with the teacher.

How do I organize my classroom to facilitate observation?

First-Grade Teacher: While creating independent learning activities, I moved away from the paper/pencil tasks I used before to keep my students busy and quiet. The quality of hands-on centers now truly engages my first graders and gives me quiet free time to observe.

Third-Grade Teacher: Ideally, I would like to have tables for students to sit at instead of their desks. I put groups of six desks together to form a working place with several independent areas for a library and writing area where either the students or I can escape to. This provides a good place to watch kids. Going and sitting at one of their working areas gives me a chance to watch them, too. I feel being at their level makes me less noticed, also. If they ask what I am up to, I'll usually tell them I'm having fun watching them learn or gaining some ideas to help me as a teacher.

Third-Grade Teacher: I've found that centers established in the classroom often create a good environment for observation. I keep reminding myself you can't observe unless your students are allowed to talk, read, and write.

What can schools and districts do to support teachers using the LR?

Third-Grade Teacher: Districts can support the schoolwide use of the LR by providing staff development time—time for workshops, time for collaboration. Districts also have to support the fact that this is a slow process and the teachers need to be supported as risk takers.

Upper-Grade teacher: Schools and districts can encourage teams of teachers to tackle the LR and provide regular and ongoing support every few weeks—at the school site.

The following list of resources needed was generated by a group of teachers using the LR:

■ Filing equipment

■ A student-free day early in the year to conduct parent-teacher interviews

■ Ungraded report cards, using performance standards

■ Two-hour language arts blocks

■ Worktables for classrooms rather than desks

■ Provision of time for teachers to collaborate with other teachers

■ Time in schedule for teacher reflection and summarizing student data

■ Staff development in authentic assessment, literature discussions, reading assessment, second language learning

■ Administration support for teacher leadership

How do I organize my records to make them easily accessible?

First-Grade Teacher: (1) clipboards with self-stick notes or "sticky" labels for anecdotal notes; (2) a binder with a tab for each student that holds observation and sample sheets; (3) hanging files accessible to students and the teacher. I tried everything to make writing observations easier. Using self-stick notes and peel-off labels required an extra step to put them in each child's folder. . . . Putting the anecdotals and sampling sheets in a binder has made my life easier. Now my notes go right on the page for each child.

Third-Grade Teacher: I have found using peel-off address labels works quite well for observations, putting the student's initials and date on them and adding them to their file. For teacher-student conferences, I have found using a tape recorder is effective. I can go back to it for reference and take any notes needed for their file. The student can go back and listen and even take it home to share. The tape is something that can have what a student shares about his or her literacy at the beginning of the year and the end of the year all on one.

Another Third-Grade Teacher: I work best with a notebook organized with a tab for each student. I also have a clipboard with labels for notes of observations. Then the labels are pasted on the student's page.

Using the Data Collection Form to Gather Evidence of Sudent Growth and Development as a Talker and Listener

The Data Collection Form provides a framework for organizing the yearlong process of collecting information about student progress. Each page of the four-page document is designed to help teachers and, as students mature, their students document selected pieces of evidence from ongoing classroom work. The evidence is then summarized in the more formal Learning Record. The following guidelines describe the intent of each section of the Data Collection Form—Talking and Listening, Reading, and Writing—with supplemental explanations and examples.

Talking and Listening

Using oral language in a variety of formal and informal social and learning environments or contexts accompanies and supports learning. Both talking and listening cut across the curriculum, through a child's investigations and observations in math, science, history/social science, and geography—and across the language modes, through talking with others as part and parcel of reading and writing activities. Within the classroom contexts, *the quality and range of experiences provided will significantly affect the child's progress and development not only as a talker and listener but also as a learner.* No performance scale for talking and listening is provided with the LR. Instead, the data collected about oral language use is reflected in the reading and writing scales.

The Social and Learning Contexts Matrix on the first page of the Data Collection Form helps teachers keep track of the range of their observations of a child using language in a variety of situations. Most observations of talk can be made informally, while working with children individually or in small groups, or by listening to children as they work on their own in pairs and in small groups. Teachers note in the space below the matrix what the child said and/or what seems significant about their observations. Quotations are best captured at the time of the observation but they can also be recorded later on.

While observing, teachers should document the ways children use their oral language to explore various experiences and how they express what they understand. Because oral expression is at the crux of learning to become literate in all subject areas, teachers must provide opportunities for partner reading, small-group discussion, presentation, and collaborative investigation so students can make the material their own. Besides, listening to what students say to each other or to themselves in the course of a classroom project is sometimes the best, most accurate assessment of what is being learned.

The observation notes allow the teacher to gather evidence to support conclusions about a child's growth and development as a talker, listener, and learner over the course of the school year. The entries teachers make in the space marked "Observations and their contexts" are brief notes or anecdotes about the child's talking, with some detail as to the context and with whom the child was talking. They date the observation so that patterns of learning can be seen. The entries are "raw data," that is, unexamined information, that describe not only what the social and learning contexts are but what the child is doing and saying within them. For example, a teacher writes:

J., a kindergartner, is working alone with pattern blocks. "Look, Ms. W., this is a pattern like blue, red, blue, red." J. points to each pattern block and goes left to right.
Teacher: "Is there another way you can describe it?"
J.: "Yeah, ABAB."
Teacher: "You already know patterns."
J.: "That's because I made a pattern!"

The two axes of the matrix reflect the *social* (horizontal) and *learning* or cognitive (vertical) contexts for talking and listening. Talk is about interaction—interaction with others and interaction with ideas—so this format links the two categories.

Social Contexts

Who we talk to affects the actual language we use. Talking with someone of a perceived higher status, for instance, can be more difficult than talking to friends and equals because it requires a more formal linguistic register. For many children, talking with an adult can be more inhibiting than talking with another child. By the same token, children need practice in this kind of speech because it calls on them to widen their socially conscious behavior and to use a more elaborated language. Talking with a friendly peer is also necessary if students are to explore ideas and reflect on what they are learning. Therefore, it is important to observe children interacting within different social situations.

The horizontal axis on the matrix suggests varied social contexts, and includes an empty box for any observation that does not fit the suggested contexts (e.g., a younger child working alone, using private speech in imaginative play).

The degree of *confidence* the child shows in a range of different situations involving expressing ideas and feelings can be noted. The child's personality will influence this, as will relationships with others in the group or pair. The child's *understanding* of and *involvement* in the topic, subject matter, or ideas being discussed, will also affect the interaction. Some children will need more support than others in contributing, through talk, to the work of the classroom. For these children, it is worthwhile to model group task talk, to pay attention to the size and composition of the learning group and to consider the cultural values associated with talk and listening.

Learning Contexts

All areas of the curriculum provide contexts for children to explore and extend their use of spoken language. It is crucial to organize the learning contexts of the classroom to give a wide range of opportunities for language use from informal to formal and from the home language or dialect to the academic language, Standard English. Additionally, it is vital to provide learning activities that support independent learning, so that you can observe the student applying *knowledge*, *skills*, and *strategies*, as well as exhibiting *confidence*, *understanding*, and *engagement* as a learner.

Some kinds of talk will come from children working collaboratively in small groups, using language to further their understanding of the learning task at hand. Other kinds of talk will be observed in a child's sharing what was learned in the

smaller group with a larger group, or the whole class.

Children need experience using language in both small and large groups. Small groups provide safe environments for exploring ideas and materials, often in quite tentative ways. They allow for close working relationships among the members of the group. Large groups provide different demands on children's talk, with a greater need for making what is being said explicit and clear for those who have not been involved in the work of the small group. Shy children and those learning English as a second language benefit, especially, from the small-group and large-group preparation and presentation times.

Listed on the vertical axis of the matrix are examples of the curriculum contexts that offer children opportunities for exploring their use of language. Empty boxes are included to add other learning contexts.

The following is a list of aspects of talk to look for, within different learning contexts.

In collaborative reading and writing activities

∎ the influence of a child's reading on his or her talk

∎ interpretations of the language of books and of word meanings

∎ appreciation of different styles in both spoken and written language

∎ a sense of the differences between spoken and written language

∎ an appreciation of subtle nuances of words (e.g., when reading and writing poetry)

∎ the ability to identify and discuss ideas that are present in a text or a story

∎ the ability to contribute positively to a group process (e.g., when writing collaboratively) and to make helpful suggestions

In play, dramatic play, drama, storytelling activities

■ children speaking in the language of the roles they are playing

■ an awareness of differences in contexts and how children change their register, dialect, and style for different contexts

■ an ability to sustain a flow of language during play and role play

■ a confidence in handling and presenting arguments and ideas while in a role

■ an ability to explore roles and issues in primary languages

■ the ways children play with language, extending and pushing the limits of what they already know, inventing new ways of saying things, and creating new plots and imagined situations in their storytelling

In curriculum areas

■ making plans for a survey, the construction of something, or an investigation of something

■ reporting on the results of a project

■ describing how something was made or the details of a journey

■ anticipating what might happen if something new is used or tried

Teacher's Role

Any assessment of a child's development and progress in talking will need to be matched against the opportunities that are provided in the classroom for that development to happen. Teachers need to search for ways to promote a child's development as a talker and listener in both informal and formal situations:

■ Consider the value of oral language in the child's culture.

■ Support the child's confidence as a talker in group situations—consider the size and the members of the group when setting up classroom experiences.

■ Analyze an activity for the opportunities it offers for using and extending language, and to anticipate the child's ability to understand the demands of the task. For development to take place, a child needs the challenge of new ideas and concepts, as well as social settings that give support for working on them.

■ Encourage a child to talk about something she or he has done or is interested in by asking open-ended questions requiring the elaborated use of language to express ideas. For example, say "Tell me what happened when you dropped the cork in the pan of water" rather than "Did the cork float when you dropped it in the pan of water?" The latter is a closed question requiring only a yes or no answer.

■ Decide how the activity can be organized so that talking and listening are necessary and the purpose of dialogue is authentic.

Using the Data Collection Form to Gather Evidence of Student Growth and Development in Reading

The Observation Notes and Reading Samples in the LR help teachers reach judgments about student reading progress. Notes and samples together provide two sources of evidence from which they can know what has been learned, what might be learned next, and what learning contexts seem most effective.

The observation notes are anecdotal perceptions of a child's developing ability in reading. What teachers learn from the observation notes can be validated or explained by analyzing actual reading samples selected as representative of student growth. These records of progress work together as supporting evidence for year-end conclusions that summarize *what a child knows and can do*, and allow for teacher placement of a child's reading development on the appropriate reading scale. "Becoming a Reader, Reading Scale 1" is used for children in Kindergarten and Grades 1 through 3. "Experience as a Reader Across the Curriculum, Reading Scale 2," is used for children in Grades 4 through 8. Both scales are provided as Appendix A.

To guide the teacher's note taking and collecting of samples, the five dimensions of learning—confidence and independence, experience, skills and strategies, knowledge and understanding, and the ability to reflect—serve as a framework through which to view all student learning. The concepts embodied in the five dimensions provide the window through which children can be observed as readers.

Reading Observations

Informal anecdotal notes, describing observed reading behaviors of a child in favorable contexts within the classroom, reveal the interconnectedness of talking and listening, and reading and writing, across a range of contexts and kinds of reading. Over time, a picture of the child's reading development emerges to corroborate and embellish information gained from the reading samples.

When writing observational notes, it is important to collect "raw data" that describes the social and learning context as well as what the child is reading, and what the child says about it. But no judgment is attached to it. For example, in a kindergarten classroom, a teacher writes the following observation about a child's reading behavior: "During center time, J. reads the room, singing the songs and chants displayed on the walls. She uses the language of the text and sometimes points to the words." Observations like this one will inform next steps for instruction and serve as evidence that the child is becoming a reader as viewed through the dimensions of learning.

Reading Samples

At least three times a year, teachers collect information about a child's reading development by observing the child read a book or text passage, using one of three different procedures—an informal reading assessment, a running record, or miscue analysis. The information gathered through these assessments is recorded on the Reading Samples portion of the LR's Data Collection Form, in response to "prompts" in the left-hand column. The prompts are reminders of what teachers need to look for to document development in reading across the dimensions of learning. The following is a description of the kinds of information to be noted as responses to the prompts.

Overall Impression of the Child's Reading

Note the *general* manner in which the child reads the selected book/text. This should include a "holistic" or overall impression of the child's reading.

Confidence and degree of independence. Comment on how the child manages the reading. Is the text difficult or easy for the child to read? Is the child willing to risk error or does he or she continually appeal for help?

Involvement in the book/text. Notice how engaged the child is in reading the text within the context of collecting the reading sample.

The way in which the child reads the text aloud. While listening to a child read, teachers can gather a wealth of information about the child as a reader. Observe if the child:

- shows enjoyment in reading orally
- reads fluently—processes "chunks" of language rather than word by word
- adjusts the reading pace to the type of text, such as for fiction or nonfiction
- uses voice intonation and expression to convey understanding and feeling

Strategies the Child Used When Reading Aloud

Drawing on previous experience to make sense of the book/text. Comment on whether the child uses prior experience or book knowledge to read the book/text. Record what the child knows about this kind of book, or, if it is a known text, what the child knows about this particular book.

Early indicators that the child is moving into reading. If the child is an emergent reader, record whether the child:

■ plays at reading by making up the story as he or she "reads"
■ focuses on the pictures to "read" the story
■ approximates the book language of a familiar text
■ looks at the print, sweeping the print with a hand, or actually tracking print with a finger, making a one-to-one correspondence.

Note whether the child can recognize words by asking if the child can find particular words after reading the text. Observe carefully to see if the child points to the requested word or rereads to locate the word. Both ways of locating are significant. If the child points automatically to the word, you know that it is a learned sight word. If the child rereads to locate the word, you know the child is developing the ability to use context to problem solve in print.

Using semantic, syntactic, and graphophonic cues. As children become more experienced readers, they begin to approach reading with the aid of three sources of information. These sources, called cueing systems, help children monitor what they read and gain meaning from the text. Comment on the child's use of the cueing systems by asking yourself the following questions as the child reads:

Does the child's reading make sense? (*Semantic* cues: meaning)

Does the child's reading sound right? (*Syntactic* cues: language structure)

Does the child's reading match the print? (*Graphophonic* cues: sound-symbol correspondence)

Consider whether *meaning drives the child's reading*—is language structure used to help work out the meaning, and is graphophonic information used to confirm meaning or to work out an unknown word?

Predicting. In learning to read and reading to learn, a child takes risks to make informed guesses based on confidence in ability, prior knowledge, and the three cueing systems. Record whether the child feels confident taking risks and making predictions about text. Also note to what extent the child uses experience and understanding of the cues to meanings in print. This is evident when the child actively searches for information by looking at the pictures (meaning), rereads or reads on (meaning and structure), and looks carefully at the print, (graphophonic). Let the child know that these strategies are important by giving the child sufficient time to try out these possibilities before offering assistance.

Self-correcting. The ability to self-correct is a significant marker in learning to read. Independence in reading begins with correcting one's own miscues. Note if the child is an active problem solver who applies reading strategies for self-correction. If meaning is lost or the text does not sound or look right, does the child look at the pictures, reread, read on, and/or look carefully at the print itself to self-correct?

Using several strategies, or overdependence on one. Good readers actively search for and use information from all the sources in an integrated fashion. Meaning can be derived from life experience and story illustrations; language structure can be derived from home and book language;

and visual and sound information can be derived from how words look and sound on the printed page. Note whether the child draws from multiple informational sources while reading, or relies heavily on only one source of information. For example, does the child read only to identify words? This behavior can be an indication of relying on visual cues as a single source.

Child's Response to the Book/Text

What a child has to say about the book/text, either during or after the reading itself, gives an insight into the child's enjoyment and personal understanding of what he or she is reading. Comment on any connections the child makes to his or her own life experiences, whether the child relates personally to the plot or characters, or shows delight in reading the book/text.

Personal response. In noting a child's response to a particular text, consider that it may be influenced by the person who chose the book/text, the amount of time allotted for browsing and reading the text beforehand, whether it is a known or unknown text, and whether the child found the story personally meaningful.

Critical response (understanding, evaluating, and appreciating wider meanings). Ask the child to recall all he or she remembers about the book/text. This requires the child to think critically about the information garnered from the text to provide a personal rendition—it engages the reader's attention on restructuring the text holistically. In the retelling, record whether the child states the main idea, recalls supporting details, and understands story sequence and/or story structure. Note if the child makes inferences within the retelling. Probe the child's deeper and wider understandings of the text by asking thinking questions which leave interpretation to the child,

such as "How do you know that?" or "What makes you think so?" With open-ended questions, you will be able to record if the child can cite experience or story details to support inferences, or make logical judgments about the author's intent and the story characters' motives and actions.

What the Sample Shows About the Child's Development as a Reader

Comment on changes in reading progress and development since the previous reading sample. Record the following types of information:

■ an ability to handle more-complex text

■ a developing ability to monitor their own comprehension by searching for information and self-correcting miscues

■ a growing involvement and interest in books

■ an increasing confidence and independence as a reader

■ a broadening interest in a range of texts

■ an ability to use reading as a way to learn across the curriculum

Experiences/Support Needed to Further Development

Record a summary of plans made for and with the child in relation to future reading experiences. These might include:

■ suggestions for further reading, ways to write about a reading, and ways to share reading with others

■ suggestions for trying new reading strategies to promote confidence and independence as a reader

■ plans for next steps in instruction

Reading Assessment Procedures

Informal Reading Assessment

An informal reading assessment provides a means for looking at a range of readers—

from emergent inexperienced readers, who may not know that the print carries the meaning, to much older and more experienced readers, who generally read silently and make few miscues while reading aloud.

Procedure

1. The child has time to browse and sample texts from a selection of fiction and nonfiction books set out by the teacher. The majority of the books in the selection are known—books that have been read during shared reading, small-group instruction, and independent reading. The teacher also includes some unknown books that are close in text complexity to the range of books the child is reading currently.

2. The child chooses the book/text passage to read.

3. The child may read the text silently to prepare for reading the text orally to the teacher.

4. The teacher and the child may preview the book together, especially if it is an unknown text. The teacher and child may read the title, discuss the illustrations, and make predictions about the text.

5. When the child is ready to read to the teacher, the teacher informs the child that he or she will be writing down on the Reading Samples log everything the child does as a reader.

6. While the child is reading, the teacher records the reading behaviors that the child exhibits, using the prompts on the Reading Samples log to structure the observations. The teacher records only what the child knows about print and the strategies the child uses to get meaning from print. In other words, the teacher notes what the child can do so that the reading samples are a chronicle of progress and development over time.

7. After the child is finished reading, the teacher and the child discuss the text and the child retells the reading in his or her own words.

8. After the assessment is completed, the teacher shares the notes with the child to reinforce confidence and independence in reading and the use of effective reading strategies.

The teacher's anecdotal notes in the Reading Samples log focus on an overall impression of the child's reading fluency, the cueing systems and strategies used by the child, and the child's response to the text. See Figure 4–1 for an example of how an informal reading assessment is recorded in the LR.

Running Records

Marie Clay developed the running record to record and analyze the reading behaviors of beginning readers. No forms or copies of the reading text are necessary to take a running

3 Reading Samples (Reading in English and/or other languages) To include reading aloud and reading silently		
Dates	12/10/96	
Title or book/text (literary or information)	Brown Bear, Brown Bear	
Known/unknown text	Known	
Sampling procedure used: informal assessment/ running record/ miscue analysis	Informal assessment	
Overall impression of the child's reading: • confidence and degree of independence • involvement in the book/text • the way in which the child reads the text aloud	Looks at pictures and chants the story in a reading-like way, using the language of the text. Acts like a reader, using concepts about print, e.g. left to right, top to botttom. Demonstrates understanding of sequence by reading across the last 2 pages.	
Strategies used when reading aloud: • drawing on previous experience to make sense of the book/text • playing at reading • using book language • reading the pictures • focusing on print (directionality, 1:1 correspondence, recognition of certain words) • using semantic, syntactic and graphophonic cues • predicting • self-correcting • using several strategies or over-dependence on one	Looks at picture on the next page to predict text on prior page; then turns back and reads "Redbird." Uses meaning/structure cues to read/ self-correct, e.g., bird/bear (sc) and orange/gold (sc). When asked what does this say-"Purple cat?", first says, "I see", looks closely and self-corrects. To the question, "How do you know that says "Purple cat?", S. says purple starts with a "p" and cat starts with a /c/.	
Child's response to the book/text: • personal response • critical response (understanding, evaluating, appreciating wider meanings	In response to what is this book all about, S. says "Animals and children and a whole bunch of stuff." Finds favorite part and tells why, "I like cats."	
What this sample shows about the child's development as a reader. Experiences/support needed to further development.	Good understanding of how books work. Enjoys books with rhyme, rhythm & repetition. Shared reading experiences to demonstrate how to integrate meaning, structure, and visual information. Ready to begin guided reading.	
* Early indicators that the child is moving into reading		

FIGURE 4–1

record. Running records are literally done by teachers "on-the-run" to capture the developing strategies of a very young reader. Recording conventions allow the teacher to map a child's reading behavior on paper as the child reads a known text.

Procedure

1. The teacher gets a copy of the book the child read the day before during instructional reading.
2. The teacher reads the title to the child and then asks the child to read the text aloud.
3. The teacher maps the child's reading behavior onto a blank sheet of paper, using the running record conventions.
4. At the end of the story the teacher comments on the meaning of the text and asks the child to retell the text in his or her own words.
5. The teacher analyzes each miscue and self-correction to determine what kind of information source(s) in the text—semantic, syntactic, graphophonic—the child uses to monitor and check the reading and to self-correct. The teacher also notes other reading behaviors observed during the running record that reveal the child's developing reading strategies (e.g., rereading, reading on, searching the picture, starting to say an unfamiliar word, making predictions, commenting, etc.).
6. The teacher divides the total number of uncorrected miscues into the total number of words in the text to determine error rate and reading accuracy. (One error out of ten to seventeen running words is within the 90 to 94 percent accuracy range, which means the text is appropriate for reading instruction purposes.
7. The teacher adds the number of uncorrected miscues and the number of self-corrections together and divides by the number of self-corrections to determine the child's self-correction rate. A good self-correction rate indicates that the child is monitoring his reading for meaning, struc-

ture, and visual match. See Clay (1993), for a complete description of scoring conventions and procedures for a running record.
8. The teacher records observations of the child's reading behavior from the running record next to the appropriate prompts on the Reading Samples log and attaches the running record and a sample of the text read by the child.

The teacher's anecdotal notes focus on the analysis of the child's reading behaviors, miscues, self-corrections, and on the level of story understanding revealed through a retelling, and the child's accuracy and self-correction rate. Through this systematic analysis, the teacher can plan what to teach next to promote strategic reading, using books within the child's instructional range. Running records over time reveal how the child is developing as a reader and moving from dependence to independence on "Becoming a Reader, Reading Scale 1."

To take a running record, the teacher uses a blank piece of paper and the running record conventions to record the child's reading behavior. At each miscue the teacher draws a horizontal line to separate the corresponding text from what the child says and/or does. Everything the child says or does is recorded above the line and everything the teacher says or does is recorded below the line directly following the corresponding text. The teacher also notes any other significant reading behaviors observed on the running record recording sheet. (See Figure 4–2 for a sample running record and Figure 4–3 for an LR Reading Sample based on it.)

Miscue Analysis

Miscue analysis is a reading assessment tool developed by Yetta Goodman et al. (1996). Myra Barrs et al. (1988) suggest that miscue analysis is most appropriate for assessing reading development when a child is a Moderately Fluent/Fluent reader on "Becoming a Reader, Reading Scale 1," and with children who are Inexperienced, Less Experienced, or

Running Record Sample:

Text: The Hungry Giant

"I want some bread!"	√√√	
Page 2 roared the giant.	√√√	
"Get me some bread,	√√√√	
or I'll hit you with my	√√√√√√	
bommy-knocker."	√√	
3 So the people ran and ran	√√√√√	
and got the giant	√√ some SC the R √	
some bread.	√√	
"I want some butter!"	√√√√	
4 roared the giant.	√√√	
"Get me some butter,	√√√ bread/butter	
or Ill hit you	√√√√	
with my bommy-knocker."	√√√√√√	
5 So the people ran and ran	√√√√√√	
and got the giant	√√√√	
some butter.	√√	
"I want some honey!"	√√√	
6 roared the giant.	√√√	
"Get me some honey,	√√√√	
or I'll hit you	√√√√	
7 with my bommy-knocker."	√√√√√√	
8 So the people ran and ran.	√√√√√√√	
They looked everywhere	√√√	
for honey.	√√	
10 "I want some honey!"	√√√	
roared the giant.	√√√	
11 "Get me	√√	
some honey!"	√√	

"Get me	√√	
some	√	
honey,	√	
12 or I'll	√√	
hit you	√√	
with	√	
my	√	
bommy-	√	
knocker." The people found a beehive.	√√√√√	
"Ah! Here is some honey,"	√ S√ Here R	√√√
13 they said,	√√ SC Here R	
and they took it	√√ look the took R it R	
to the giant.	√√√	
"Here is some honey,"	√√√√	
14 they said.	√√	
The giant looked at	√√√√	
the beehive.	√√	
"That's not honey!"	This That's T	√√ R
he said,	√√	
15 and he hit it	√√√√	
with his	√√	
bommy-knocker.	√√ "It's not 'after.'"
The bees zoomed out.	√√√ after A out T
They zoomed at the giant.	They √√√√
16 "Ow!" he roared,	√ R√ √
and he ran and ran,	√√√√√
"ow, ow, OW,"	ouch ouch ouch SC SC
all the way home.	ow ow ow R All √√√

Analysis

183	running words	Error Rate	1:30	6 errors + 5 SC	
6	errors	Accuracy	97 %	5 SC	= 1:2

FIGURE 4–2

3 Reading Samples (Reading in English and/or other languages) To include reading aloud and reading silently		
Dates	December 9, 1996	
Title or book/text (literary or information)	The Hungry Giant	
Known/unknown text	Known (yesterday's new book)	
Sampling procedure used: informal assessment/ running record/ miscue analysis	Running record	
Overall impression of the child's reading: • confidence and degree of independence • involvement in the book/text • the way in which the child reads the text aloud	C. reads with fluency and good phrasing. He makes his voice sound like the giant's when reading enlarged text.	
Strategies used when reading aloud: • drawing on previous experience to make sense of the book/text • playing at reading • using book language • reading the pictures • focusing on print (directionality, 1:1 correspondence, recognition of certain words) • using semantic, syntactic and graphophonic cues • predicting • self-correcting • using several strategies or over-dependence on one	C. uses meaning and structure and the beginning part of a word to predict text. He self-corrects if there isn't a visual match, and if he "knows" the word. C. attempts to correct an unknown word by rereading. He isn't successful, but knows that rereading can help him, e.g., This/That's/T C. notices a discrepancy—after/out "It's not after."/T. (See attached running record.)	
Child's response to the book/text: • personal response • critical response (understanding, evaluating, appreciating wider meanings)	C. thinks the giant acted mean because he was hungry.	
What this sample shows about the child's development as a reader. **Experiences/support needed to further development.**	C. reads more complex text with a higher rate of accuracy. More consistent at noticing discrepancies. Help C. learn to link from known to unknown words, and to look for known chunks in unknown words.	

* Early indicators that the child is moving into reading

FIGURE 4–3

Moderately Experienced readers on "Experience as a Reader Across the Curriculum, Reading Scale 2."

Miscue analysis, like running records, is a process that teachers use to observe, record, and analyze the reading behaviors of children to determine if they are developing effective reading strategies that promote confident, independent, fluent readers across a range of reading contexts. Recording conventions are used to map the child's reading behavior onto a photocopy of the text passage that the child is reading. Although miscue analysis has been slightly adapted for the Learning Record, the intent is to be true to the principles established by the author.

Preparing Text Selections

1. The teacher selects unknown or not-well-known texts that will be challenging enough that the child will make miscues that allow for teacher observation of the child's reading strategies, but not so difficult that it causes the child to be frustrated. It is best to have several texts available, so if the child has difficulty or reads one text too easily, another one can be chosen.

2. The teacher chooses and photocopies passages of 150 to 300 words from the middle of the texts that have a sense of completeness, such as a short chapter or a section from a nonfiction book. Whole and complete passages that use natural language patterns, have strong narrative or expository structures, and contain pictures or diagrams are best.

Procedure

1. The teacher tells the child the purpose of the reading conference—to note what the child does as a reader when reading unknown or not-well-known text silently

and aloud, and how well the child can discuss/retell what he or she reads after both the silent and oral readings.

2. Sometimes the teacher gives the child the book and indicates the passage to be read silently.

3. The teacher records the reading behaviors she or he observes while the child reads the text silently (e.g., subvocalization, how long the silent reading is sustained, the degree of involvement, the amount of independence demonstrated).

4. The teacher asks the child to retell the passage in his or her own words, while the teacher records notes about the child's understanding of the text as a direct result of the silent reading.

5. The teacher asks the child to read the passage aloud without assistance. The teacher might say, "I would like you to read this part of the book aloud. If you come to a word or phrase you don't understand or know, do what you would normally do if you were reading alone."

6. If the child asks for help, the teacher encourages the child to try to figure it out.

7. The teacher records the miscues and what the child does when he or she encounters difficulty or contradiction in the passage.

8. The teacher asks the child to talk about the passage in more detail, using open-ended, probing questions about characters, setting, events, plot, or theme for narrative text and questions about major concepts, generalizations, specific information, and logical structuring if the passage is from an expository text.

The teacher's anecdotal notes focus on the analysis of the miscues to determine their positive and negative influence on the child's ability to gain meaning from unknown or not-well-known text, and to determine the overall understanding of the passage. The teacher uses the observations from the miscue analysis to record responses to the prompts on the Reading Samples log and attaches the miscue analysis.

Sampling a child's miscues and level of comprehension after a silent and oral reading of unknown or not-well-known texts helps the teacher plan for instruction to support the child in becoming an experienced reader across a range of literary genres.

See Figure 4–4 for an annotated list of the behaviors to look for in a child's reading of the prepared text as well as the conventional way to note it. The prepared text used in this example is taken from the analysis of a complete miscue sample for Sally, a fourth-grade student whose first language is English. Figures 4–5 and 4–6 exemplify the way a text was marked for that child and the way the consequent LR reading sample was composed.

Miscue Analysis Conventions

Substitutions: The word substituted is written above the corresponding word in the text.

Look, said Billy to himself, staring [starting] down at the fried worm

Repetitions: Text that is repeated is underlined. More than one underline denotes the number of times the text is repeated.

He's like that.

Insertions: The inserted word is written above an insertion mark.

He eggs other people on, but never [he] wants to do anything himself.

Omissions: The text omitted is circled.

Tom (was) just scared. [sat]

Reversals: An editor's transposition symbol indicates which words have been read in reverse.

"Give up?" asked Alan.

Self-correction: A circled C is written next to the miscue.

For the first time he wondered what [that ©] he'd do [did] if he lost.

FIGURE 4–4

Chapter XII THE FIFTH WORM

Look, said Billy to himself, staring down at the fried worm on the plate. Be sensible. How can it hurt me? I've eaten four already. Tom was just scared. He's like that. He eggs other people on, but never wants to do anything himself.

"Give up?" asked Alan.

"Come on," said Joe. "We haven't got all day."

"Five more minutes," said Alan. "Then I win."

"There's no time limit," said Billy. For the first time he wondered what he'd do if he lost. Where could he ever get fifty dollars? But how could he eat ten *more* ? Big, fat, ugly, soft, brown things. He couldn't ask his father for fifty dollars.

He heard Alan and Joe whispering together.

"He's gonna quit."

"Yeah. I knew he'd never make it when I bet with him. He talks big. Him and Tom are just the same. But they never *do* anything."

Billy gritted his teeth, glopped on ketchup, mustard, salt, grated cheese; whatever was on the crate, anything, everything, and then grabbed up the worm and tore it apart with his hands, stuffing it into his mouth, chewing and chewing and swallowing, gulping..

Then, panting, he reached out and wiped his gooey hands on Alan's trousers and grinned messily up at him and said,

"There. Five."

Analysis of Miscues: Retained meaning: 8   Lost meaning: 8

FIGURE 4–5

3 Reading Samples (Reading in English and/or other languages)
To include reading aloud and reading silently

Dates	9/23/97
Title or book/text (literary or information)	How to Eat Fried Worms. Chapter XII: The Fifth Worm.
Known/unknown text	Unknown, but read silently to prepare
Sampling procedure used: informal assessment/ running record/ miscue analysis	Miscue Analysis
Overall impression of the child's reading: • confidence and degree of independence • involvement in the book/text • the way in which the child reads the text aloud	Text is fairly easy to read. Reads with expression. Slows down when text is difficult. Takes risks to figure out unknown words independently; doesn't appeal.
Strategies used when reading aloud: • drawing on previous experience to make sense of the book/text • playing at reading • using book language • reading the pictures • focusing on print (directionality, 1:1 correspondence, recognition of certain words) • using semantic, syntactic and graphophonic cues • predicting • self-correcting • using several strategies or over-dependence on one	Monitors reading for overall visual match and about half the time for meaning. Successfully self-corrects miscues containing known words, e.g. what/that, he/his, Tom/him. Uses beginning and ending chunks of words to decode unknown words and confuses words with similar visual configuration, e.g. grated/gritted, now/how. Not concerned if meaning is lost or if the word is a nonsense word, e.g. gridded/grinned.
Child's response to the book/text: • personal response • critical response (understanding, evaluating, appreciating wider meanings	Before reading aloud, gives main idea of story. Understands story at a literal level, "They think he should just quit because they don't have all day and he won't eat the sixth worm."Confuses characters.
What this sample shows about the child's development as a reader. Experiences/support needed to further development.	Reading more complex text. Use graphic organizers to show chapter book structure. Retell, discuss & predict before /after reading parts of a novel. Sample reading daily to prompt to meaning when making miscues that lose meaning.

* Early indicators that the child is moving into reading

FIGURE 4–6

Resources

The references used in this section of the handbook are listed in the References section, pages 99–100. Teachers would do well to read the original sources to gain a fuller understanding of the reading assessment methods described.

Using the Data Collection Form to Gather Evidence of Student Growth and Development in Writing

When the focus of assessment is on collecting evidence that students are becoming fluent and experienced writers, the task begins with providing opportunities for students to write. Teachers can encourage children's development as writers by providing a range and variety of experiences, within a variety of social and learning contexts. Children need the opportunity to write in many genres for authentic purposes, including the opportunity to write in all areas of the curriculum on a regular, daily basis. The LR helps teachers and their students keep track of progress as they engage in normal and ongoing classroom writing activities.

Just as they do in collecting evidence of growth for each child as a reader, teachers use the five dimensions of learning—confidence and independence, experience, skills and strategies, knowledge and understanding, and the ability to reflect—as a framework through which to view students as writers. The concepts embodied in the five dimensions are integral to what teachers include in the LR writing samples and observations.

Writing Observations

The observation notes are a teacher's anecdotal perceptions of a child's developing ability in writing. They are portraits of moments in learning that stand out to the teacher as significant examples of growth. The teacher collects "raw data," recording the social and learning context as well as anything the child says or does that reflects growth across the five dimensions of learning. For example, one first-grade teacher writes, "During activity time, J. finds the class book, *The Ouch Book*. J. draws a picture. Says to teacher, 'I need help with the words.' Teacher says, 'I bet you can do it all on your own. Say the words and write the sounds you hear.' J. smiles and writes, I BT MY TN (I bit my tongue) independently. Reads it back and points to the words. Shares it at story time."

Writing Samples

At least three times a year, the teacher collects information about a child's writing development by looking at a selected writing sample. The sample, chosen by the child or the child and the teacher, is discussed together. The information gathered from the writing conference is recorded on the Writing Samples page of the Data Collection Forms, as responses to "prompts" in the left-hand column. The prompts are reminders of what to look for to document progress and development in writing, across the dimensions of learning. It is important to keep the child's writing, either the original pieces or photocopies, with the Writing Samples page, so that they may be referred to when preparing a year-end summary of student achievement and for moderation purposes.

Prompts on the Writing Samples Page

Context and Background Information About the Writing   Record the social context, learning context, and the strategies the child used to accomplish the writing task. Consider the following as you analyze the writing sample:

How the writing arose. Note whether the writing topic was assigned or self-chosen, what the curriculum context was, and if the writing was a response to something observed, discussed, or read.

How the child went about the writing. How long did the child work on it? Did the child write more than one draft?

Whether the child was writing alone or with others. Record the social context of the sample.

Whether the writing was discussed with anyone while the child was working on it. Note the level of support given to the child and if she or he responded to any suggestions offered by others.

What kind of writing it is. Along with noting the kind of writing (e.g., story, journal entry, report), comment on what type of voice the writer used. Was it an expressive, personal voice, which reflects self-confidence, or was it a voice taken from reading text, which reveals the writer's growing experience and sense of story or genre?

Whether the writing is a complete piece of work or an extract. The sample chosen may be a complete piece of writing or an extract from a lengthy piece of writing, such as a chapter book. Also note whether the sample is a final draft or a rough draft that will be worked on further.

Child's Own Response to the Writing

Record the child's own comments about the piece of writing. Invite the child to reflect on:

■ how the child decided on the choice of topic or what the writing is about

■ if the child had a plan for how the writing was to be laid out on the paper (design for genre and structure)

■ what the child likes best about the piece of writing

■ what this piece of writing shows about the child as a writer

Teacher's Response

To the content of the writing. Note whether the writing has meaning for the intended reader and is clear, honest, informative, and interesting.

To the child's ability to handle this particular kind of writing. Comment on the child's confidence using the appropriate form and structure (organization, sequencing, and arrangement) for this kind of writing and if the kind of writing fits the audience and purpose.

Overall impressions. Record any general impressions you might have about the particular writing sample. This should be a "holistic" view of the child's development as a writer.

Development of Spelling and Conventions of Writing

Comment on the child's range of strategies for using and spelling written language. Analyze what the piece of writing shows about the child's understanding of the writing system and note any patterns of development and progress:

Is the spelling conventional? Does the writing show evidence of identifying and correcting misspelled words?

Is the child using temporary spellings for unknown words? Are these spellings good guesses?

Is the child developing a visual awareness of spelling patterns and common letter combinations?

Record what the writing sample shows about the child's knowledge and understanding of how to present written language to the reader:

Does the child know how to lay out the text?

Does the child mark sentences with appropriate punctuation?

Does the child use appropriate paragraph form and structure?

Are the sentences well connected and varied?

Is the vocabulary appropriate for the kind of writing: narrative, descriptive, or informational?

What This Writing Shows About the Child's Development as a Writer

How it fits into the range of the child's previous writing. Record any important changes you notice about the child's writing since the last time you completed a writing sample. Consider the following signs of development:

■ growing pleasure and involvement in writing

■ increasing confidence and independence as a writer

■ drawing on reading experiences to extend the range of writing

■ increasing ability to work for longer periods of time, writing more extended and complex texts

■ increasing ability to revise own writing by making the necessary changes, deletions, expansions, and corrections to make the writing meaningful, clear, and informative to the reader

Note if the child's range as a writer in English and/or other languages is widening. Is the writing sample representative of the kind of writing the child does? If so, does it indicate a new development in knowledge and understanding of the text form for this kind of writing? Or, is the child trying out a new kind of writing, voice, or style not previously attempted?

Experiences/support needed to further development. Record a summary of plans made *for and with the child* in relation to future writing experiences. These might include:

■ ways the child can share his or her writing with other children and adults

■ suggestions for further reading experiences that exemplify the style or genre the child is currently developing

■ plans for next steps in instruction

What teachers learn from the observation notes is validated by analyzing actual writing samples selected as representative of student achievement. These records of student progress all work together as supporting evidence for year-end conclusions that summarize *what a child knows and can do*, and allow teachers to determine where each child is as a writer on "Writing Scale 1: Becoming a Writer" for children in kindergarten through Grade 3, and "Writing Scale 2: Becoming Experienced as a Writer" for children in Grades 4 through 8. (See the Writing Scales in Appendix A.)

A writing sample of a fourth-grade student whose first language is Spanish but who chose to write in English can be seen as Figure 4–7. The sample includes a copy of the student's writing from her portfolio of work, Figure 4–8, and the information needed for both teacher and student to understand its significance in her progress as a developing writer. With three such samples and observation notes gathered over the course of the year, the teacher can note a pattern of progress that can be summarized in Part B3.

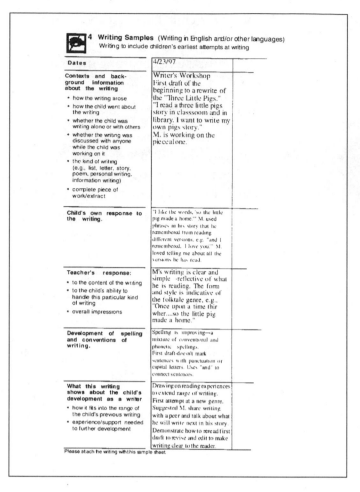

FIGURE 4–7

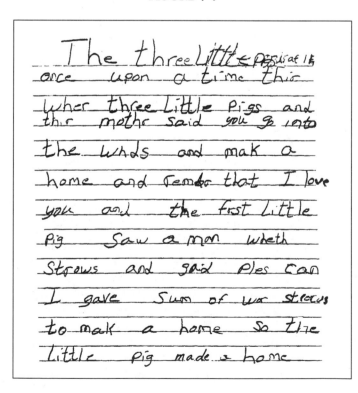

FIGURE 4–8

Professional Development

As teachers involve themselves in efforts to improve student achievement, they need better information on student learning than they have had in the past. Many find that, as they reform their curriculum and instruction, what they learn from standard measures about what their students know and can do is inadequate. Pertinent data about student progress throughout the year becomes essential if they are to assess the extent and quality of such progress and, what's more, provide the kinds of opportunities students must have to reach the next stage of development.

What It Takes to Improve Student Learning

To improve student achievement, well-prepared teachers must use effective teaching methods. Although these methods have been identified by research and best practice, they are not in widespread use in classrooms. Effective approaches include interactive, thought-provoking activities among students with teachers across the curriculum, oral and written dialogue in every subject to build language and literacy skills, and the reconception of school as a place that con-

nects instruction to students' strengths and everyday experiences in their homes and communities.

Staff development for this complex kind of teaching requires that teachers have time to develop expertise in collecting and analyzing data about what and how their students are learning. Teachers find that such rich information improves their own teaching because it highlights just how they can help their students learn. They need to join with both colleagues and administrators in ongoing joint reviews of student work, however, if they are to use the information fully and effectively. Through systematic, sustained staff development, the Learning Record provides a framework for teachers to collaborate across grade levels and subject areas to revise classroom and school assessment practices. The time required to review student work samples in terms of set standards is a necessary investment. The LR moderations of student records by site staffs to calibrate their interpretations of site standards provide for self-evaluation of school programs and individual student progress, validated by a quality assurance system of assessment. (See Sadler's description of the LR system in the Introduction.) At the same time that teachers review student records of achievement, they are also expanding their instructional approaches. A two-for-one benefit accrues: a strong classroom assessment that reaches from classroom to other classrooms and back again, and a professional development program based on what teachers need to know in order to help their students improve their achievement.

The LR Approach Validates and Strengthens the Teacher's Role in Assessment

With the LR, unlike with traditional testing schemes, it is the classroom teachers who take responsibility for documenting demonstrations of student learning and for evaluating what the documentation means in terms of meeting set standards. When teachers write summaries of the information they have collected about student performance throughout the year, they are doing the necessary analysis to arrive at sound judgments about what standards have been attained and what are next to learn or teach. This process of interpreting and summarizing data and using set standards is the assessment process itself. Consistent with good scientific practice, the LR summaries of parent and student observation (Part A), the summaries of observations and samples of work collected throughout the year (Part B), and the update summaries from all participants in the assessment (Part C) provide evidence from multiple sources for the trustworthy appraisal of student performance.

Appropriate for all students in all kinds of classroom configurations, the LR is especially constructive in assessing student progress in multilevel classes. It addresses the wide range of abilities, experience, and needs of students at risk of failure (e.g., children of the poor, Title 1 students, migrant students, special education students, and English language learners) by providing avenues for teachers to learn about and respond to the often concealed or misinterpreted scholastic and personal strengths of those outside mainstream cultures. By providing for individual records of achieve-

ment, LR teachers find that they can also challenge and support those who excel academically.

How the LR Program Works to Inform Teachers and Their Assessments

To ensure that teachers become responsible for a classroom-based student assessment that can be held up to public scrutiny, they need to be able to rely on a sustained professional development program that will allow them to phase in the LR. The following schedule is typical:

1. *First year of LR use:* A cadre of faculty leaders or the whole staff voluntarily complete three to five records in order to learn the assessment system. These teachers lead expansion of LR use within their schools by modeling the process.

2. *Second year:* Faculty leaders expand LR use across the school and develop site exemplars for each grade level. A baseline of student reading achievement at each grade level can be drawn and used to measure progress in subsequent year.

3. *Third year and beyond:* Individual students are assessed as meeting or exceeding grade-specific performance standards in reading and writing. Reports for all or target groups of students are available for school staffs, students, and their parents, with literacy scores annually validated as consistent and fair.

Teachers Meet in Seminar to Phase in the LR

A series of seminars, held at a school or at a regional site under the auspices of the Center for Language in Learning (see p.xii for a description of the Center), supports teachers interested in beginning or furthering their use of the LR in their own classrooms and schools. Customized schedules distribute the seminars throughout the year for a minimum of thirty-five hours for each of the first two years. (After two years, enough teacher leadership has usually been developed at the school that only fifteen to twenty hours is required for CLL-led LR seminars. The school faculty as a whole annually reviews a sample of student records using the LR moderation process.)

During the initial seminars, teachers discuss each part of the LR, try it out with their own students, and then share their findings with colleagues at the next session. An LR teacher, certified by the Center, guides the seminars, coaches the staff, and conducts the official review of student records. In addition to this seminar leader or coach, school registration with the Center provides resource materials and methods of assessment, the conduct of school and regional moderations to validate classroom and site judgments, and school-level reports of student achievement. Certified LR teacher-coaches represent all grade levels and many schools and districts across the United States.

Seminar topics for a six-day or thirty-five-hour series during the first year include the following:

❚ techniques for interviewing parents and students about student learning and goals

❚ use of the five dimensions of learning to observe and document students' reading and writing

❚ classroom and record management

❚ guided practice in moderating student record exemplars and summarizing data

❚ site and intersite moderations of student records from participants' classes

Seminar topics after the first year are based on site faculty needs related to (1) providing validation for consistent, trustworthy judgments of student achievement, and (2) improving student achievement.

Teachers Reflect on Their First Year with the LR

The LR supports the kinds of curriculum and instruction recommended in research and best practice as required for assessing student attainment of standards. It is, however, a dramatically different kind of standardized assessment from the norm-referenced tests that teachers, not to mention parents and students, are used to. Teachers typically report that their own growth as professionals increases when they incorporate this new vision of assessment into their own teaching styles and subject matter contents. Typically, the question "Why use the Learning Record?" elicits reflections like these:

It's authentic; we're looking at what kids can really do.

It drives our curriculum. We have a sense of what work looks like if a student is performing at the level of a 4 or 5 on the performance scale. Helps us set standards.

Forces me to focus on what kids expect of themselves.

The performance scales have instructional implications.

Facilitates metacognitive [learning], which we need to do to produce lifelong learners.

Helps students, parents, teachers see what the student has learned and what he or she needs to do to develop and grow.

This assessment values the student as a learner, the classroom curriculum, and the professionalism of the teacher.

Becoming a Learning Record Teacher

The previous reflections were written at the end of the first year of professional development for the LR. Tammy, Pat, and Joan wrote the following reflections at the end of each of the first three seminars. These reflections, typical of the evolution of feelings expressed, are given to remind us that focusing on student progress according to set standards represents a major change for most teachers. Therefore, it cannot happen overnight, and it requires belief in the value of informed teacher judgment as an important part of improving student achievement.

Tammy

Tammy, for example, struggled to comprehend how she could work harder than she already was working to make the changes she decided she must make.

12/7: As I sit here I feel so overwhelmed. There is so much information to remember. I enjoy the interviews and I like observing the children. I believe you learn a lot by "kidwatching." I get frustrated sometimes because I want to help every child, but I don't always go about it the right way. I feel that I am not doing enough for the children. This observing will help me know more about my children and maybe give some insight into their problems.

2/12: It seems like a lot of work. I don't always find the time to do a lot of observing. It seems like our system of language arts is going to have to change. I have received a lot of ideas from group discussions during these seminars to take back to my classroom that have been very helpful. Right now I feel very overwhelmed. The information is given to us quickly. It takes time to digest.

3/14: Now I understand that parents can be concerned about their child even if they don't come for a conference. I also spend more time watching my students so I can learn more about what they can do. As a teacher, I always need to focus on things that can be changed to make learning more valuable for the children.

Pat

Pat, a special education teacher, was encouraged by his participation in LR seminars to rethink the curriculum and the impact it was having on his students. He describes how, over a three-month period, the LR challenged him to face these issues and then rewarded him with a more thorough understanding of his students as learners.

2/1: As an LH teacher using [a commercial skills-based program], I find that my students must read passages within a time limit with no more than a small number of errors. This process focuses on errors and does not focus on meaning. Many of my students would be further along in the series if it focused on meaning. The Special Education Department mandates the teaching of literature as well as [the program]. However, because of time constraints, we are lucky to do the literature series for one hour each week. I must become more creative in my use of time to include literature more regularly and focus on meaning-based reading strategies.

3/14: I am coming to terms with my reluctance to commit my observations to the LR. Knowing that other teachers are facing the same questions and trusting this experiment should help me follow through better.

5/2: This process has helped me to focus more clearly on the language development process. The final LR product really shows a rounded picture of the child. I also found that the group process (staff development) helped me to refine my observations to "show" rather than evaluate. The parent involvement was invaluable as I opened the door to forming a partnership with parents in helping the child develop as a language learner. I saw writing produced for cub scouts, personal reasons, and church-related activities. I would have never seen how my students understood the power of words without this input. This also enabled time to expand my teaching.

Joan

Often, when teachers begin to experiment with the LR in their classrooms, they begin to question traditional assessment practices that have been embedded in the educational system for decades. Joan questions the traditional separation of assessment and learning. She challenges her own teaching practice in favor of the new practice, which she now controls, to help her students learn and to include parents in the process.

12/3: I am still in a stage of confusion and uncertainty about many aspects of this program. I enjoy the conference with the parent and being able to focus on positive activities. I thought the parent was made more aware of the importance of "nonschool" activities that contributed to the child's learning.

I found doing report cards extremely frustrating this year. I know that many parents equate assessment with the concept of letter grades and use them to label children. In parent conferences I explained how difficult it was to assign a letter grade to the kind of work children were doing in my classroom. I did emphasize as many positives as possible and the importance of the role of the parent in the child's education.

2/10: Finding the time to do the LR and rearranging our schedule seems to be my primary

goal. I don't have to worry about justifying what I am doing to the site administration. My students' parents are supportive of the process.

3/15: I really feel that I have a beginning of a new way to assess my students. Next year I am going to use LR as one of my evaluation objectives. Perhaps I will use just the reading portion, but with my whole class. If that becomes too overwhelming, I might just use the observation and sample part. Whatever I decide, I will make it part of my weekly schedule and hope it will become a habit that my class and I develop. I need to organize my classroom, myself, and my students in a way that will make this assessment a regular part of the day. When I do this, I will be able to see where my students are in their development and find ways to help them move toward the next level.

The following two scales are used with the LR to describe the development of reading in elementary and middle school students. Two more scales describe writing development stages.

Reading Scales

Reading Scale 1 (the "Becoming a Reader" scale used in Kindergarten to Grade 3) assists teachers in describing reading development as students move from dependence to independence. The characteristics at each level on the scale describe what students are progressively able to do in the process of becoming fluent readers.

Particulars about students' increasing abilities to read grade-level texts, both literature and nonliterature, with ease and fluency will need to be included in the Part B summaries of student progress, based on such classroom data as student responses to their reading and teacher observations of oral discussions or drawings about their reading.

Reading Scale 2 (used in Grades 4 through 8) focuses on the student's involvement with a wide range and variety of reading material. The teacher documents the student's journey from a limited experience with print through deep and broad engagement in text as a reader across the curriculum.

Specific evidence demonstrating the extent to which students can understand a wide variety of both grade-level texts and self-selected books and magazines will need to be included in student portfolios, reading logs, and in written responses to their reading and documented observations of oral discussions of their reading.

Writing Scales

Writing Scale 1 (the "Becoming a Writer" scale used in Kindergarten to Grade 3) focuses the teacher on the characteristics of the developing student writer—from the physical act of putting oral language on paper, chalkboard, or computer screen to the actual use of writing to communicate meaning. The scale integrates the transcription and the composing aspects of writing as one supports and reinforces the other. This scale describes six stages of development.

Writing Scale 2 (a "Writing Experience" scale used in Grades 4 through 8) parallels the reading scale for this grade span in emphasizing breadth of experience with all kinds of writing and a full range of audiences for the writer to address.

With writing, as with reading assessment, students should collect their writing all year in portfolios of their work. A range of writing for a variety of purposes, on both assigned and self-chosen topics, can then be sampled periodically for signs of progress and information for instruction.

NOTE: Bilingual students can become readers in more than one language; therefore, a student may be at one point on the scale in the primary language and at another point in learning the second (or third) language. Both can be documented with the LR by using the Language 1 and Language 2 arrows on the scales.

READING SCALE 1, GRADES K–3: BECOMING A READER

Dependence   **Independence**

Language 1

Language 2

1	2	3	4	5
Beginning Reader	**Not-Yet-Fluent Reader**	**Moderately Fluent Reader**	**Fluent Reader**	**Exceptionally Fluent Reader**
Uses just a few successful strategies for tackling print independently. Relies on having another person to read the text aloud. May still be unaware that text carries meaning.	Tackling known and predictable text with growing confidence but still needing support with new and unfamiliar ones. Growing ability to predict meanings and developing strategies to check predictions against other cues such as the illustrations and the print itself.	Well-launched on reading but still needs to return to a familiar range of reader text. At the same time beginning to explore new kinds of texts independently. Beginning to read silently.	A capable reader who now approaches familiar texts with confidence but still needs support with unfamiliar materials. Beginning to draw inferences from books and stories. Reads independently. Chooses to read silently.	An avid and independent reader who is making choices from a wider range of material. Able to appreciate nuances and subtlety in text.

Published as a component of The Learning Record Assessment System™ . For further information, call or write the Center for Language in Learning at 10610 Quail Canyon Road, El Cajon, CA 92021; (619) 443-6320. Adapted with permission from the Primary Language Record (PLR), developed and copyrighted by the Centre for Language in Primary Education, Webber Row Teachers Centre, Webber Row, London SE1 8QW, in 1988 and distributed in the United States by Heinemann. ISBN 0-435-08516-6.

READING SCALE 2, GRADES 4–8: BECOMING EXPERIENCED IN READING

Dependence   **Independence**

Language 1

Language 2

1	2	3	4	5
Inexperienced	**Less Experienced**	**Moderately Experienced**	**Experienced**	**Exceptionally Experienced**
Experience as a reader has been limited. Generally chooses to read a very easy and familiar text where illustrations play an important part. Has difficulty with any unfamiliar materials and yet may be able to read own dictated texts confidently. Needs a great deal of support with the reading demands of the classroom. Overdependent on one strategy when reading aloud, often reads word by word. Rarely chooses to read for pleasure.	Developing fluency as a reader and reading certain kinds of material with confidence. Usually chooses short books with simple narrative shapes and with illustrations. May read these silently; often rereads favorite books. Reading for pleasure often includes comics and magazines. Needs help with the reading demands of the classroom and especially with using reference and information books.	A confident reader who feels at home with books. Generally reads silently and is developing stamina as a reader. Is able to read for longer periods and cope with more demanding texts, including novels. Willing to reflect on reading and often uses reading in own learning. Selects books independently and can use information books and materials for straightforward reference purposes, but still needs help with unfamiliar material, particularly nonnarrative prose.	A self-motivated, confident, and experienced reader who may be pursuing particular interests through reading. Capable of tackling some demanding texts and can cope well with the reading of the curriculum. Reads thoughtfully and appreciates shades of meaning. Capable of locating and drawing on a variety of sources in order to research a topic independently.	An enthusiastic and reflective reader who has strong established tastes in fiction and nonfiction. Enjoys pursuing own reading interests independently. Can handle a wide range and variety of texts, including some adult material. Recognizes that different kinds of text require different styles of reading. Able to evaluate evidence drawn from a variety of information sources. Is developing critical awareness as a reader.

Published as a component of The Learning Record Assessment System™. For further information, call or write the Center for Language in Learning at 10610 Quail Canyon Road, El Cajon, CA 92021; (619) 443-6320. Adapted with permission from the Primary Language Record (PLR), developed and copyrighted by the Centre for Language in Primary Education, Webber Row Teachers Centre, Webber Row, London SE1 8QW, in 1988 and distributed in the United States by Heinemann. ISBN 0-435-08516-6.

WRITING SCALE 1, GRADES K–3: BECOMING A WRITER

Dependence ← Language 1

Language 2

Independence →

1 Beginning Writer	2 Early Writer	3 Developing Writer	4 Moderately Fluent Writer	5 Fluent Writer	6 Exceptionally Fluent Writer
May be composing by dictating own texts, and may have some strategies for writing independently (e.g., drawing, writing, copying, inventing own code), but still at an early stage of understanding how language is written down, and needing support with transcription.	Gaining confidence in using writing for a range of personal purposes (e.g., messages, notices). Drawing on experiences of seeing language written down (e.g., in shared writing), and demonstrating more understanding of the alphabetic nature of the English writing system. Ready to try writing independently, using a few early strategies for spelling (e.g., use of initial letters, some known words, using letter strings as "place holders" so that writing can be read back more consistently).	Using a small range of writing (e.g, letters, lists, brief narratives), independently, but still needing help with extending and developing texts. May be drawing on models from reading in structuring own texts. Reading back own texts consistently, experimenting with punctuation, and developing strategies for spelling (e.g., known words, phonetically based spellings), which enable texts to be read by others.	Writing more confidently and developing ideas at greater length in a few familiar forms. Growing ability to structure these texts; willing to experiment with a wider range of writing. Beginning to use punctuation to support meaning (e.g., periods, exclamation marks). Drawing on a wider range of strategies in spelling (e.g., common letter strings), awareness of visual patterns as well as phonetically based spellings.	Growing independence in using writing for a wide range of purposes (e.g., expressive, informational, imaginative). Aware of different audiences and beginning to shape texts for a reader. Often chooses to write over longer periods. Punctuating texts for meaning more consistently. Writing shows increasing attention to the visual patterns in spelling.	A confident and independent writer who enjoys writing in different genres and is developing a personal voice. Writing may show marked influences of texts that have been read. Drawing on a range of effective strategies for spelling and using standard forms more consistently. Using written language in more deliberate ways and making meanings explicit. Still needs support in sustaining long pieces of writing or expressing complex meanings.

Published as a component of The Learning Record Assessment System™. For further information, call or write the Center for Language in Learning at 10610 Quail Canyon Road, El Cajon, CA 92021; (619) 443-6320. Adapted with permission from the Primary Language Record (PLR), developed and copyrighted by the Centre for Language in Primary Education, Webber Row Teachers Centre, Webber Row, London SE1 8QW, in 1988 and distributed in the United States by Heinemann. ISBN 0-435-08516-6.

WRITING SCALE 2, GRADES 4–8: BECOMING EXPERIENCED AS A WRITER

Inexperienced   Experienced

Language 1

Language 2

1 Inexperienced	2 Less Experienced	3 Moderately Experienced	4 Experienced	5 Exceptionally Experienced
Experience as a writer may be limited: may compose orally with confidence but be reluctant to write or take risks with transcription. Needs a great deal of help with developing own texts (which are often brief and formulaic) and the writing demands of the classroom. Relies mainly on phonetic spelling strategies and memorized words, with few strategies for self-help. Seldom uses punctuation to mark meaning.	More willing to take risks with both composition and transcription. Writes confidently in certain genres (e.g., simple narratives), often willing to try out different forms of writing, drawing on experience of the models available. May find it difficult to sustain initial efforts over longer pieces of writing. Mainly uses language and sentence structures that are close to speech. Spellings of familiar words are generally correct and attempts at unfamiliar words reveal a widening range of spelling strategies. Uses sentence punctuation more consistently.	Shaping writing in familiar genres confidently, drawing on experience of reading. Widening range of writing and taking on different forms more successfully. Aware of audience and beginning to consider appropriateness of language and style. Learning to revise own texts with support and to link and develop ideas coherently. Spellings of words with regular patterns are mainly correct and attempts at unfamiliar words show a growing knowledge of visual patterns and word structures. Uses sentence punctuation appropriately.	A self-motivated writer who can write at length and is beginning to use writing to refine own ideas. Developing own style and range as a writer but needs support with the structuring of more complex narrative and nonnarrative forms. Likely to reflect on writing and to revise texts for a reader, choosing language for effect or to clarify meanings. Using standard spelling more consistently and drawing on effective self-help strategies. Increasingly able to use punctuation, including paragraphing, to organize texts.	An enthusiastic writer who has a recognizable voice and who uses writing as a tool for thinking. Making conscious decisions about appropriate forms and styles of writing, drawing on wide experience of reading. May show marked preferences for particular genres. Able to craft texts with the reader in mind and reflect critically on own writing. Using mostly standard spelling. Managing extended texts using organizational structures such as paragraphing and headings.

Published as a component of The Learning Record Assessment System™. For further information, call or write the Center for Language in Learning at 10610 Quail Canyon Road, El Cajon, CA 92021; (619) 443-6320. Adapted with permission from the Primary Language Record (PLR), developed and copyrighted by the Centre for Language in Primary Education, Webber Row Teachers Centre, Webber Row, London SE1 8QW, in 1988 and distributed in the United States by Heinemann. ISBN 0-435-08516-6.

The following scale was developed by Hilary Hester as a member of the staff at the Centre for Language in Primary Education. The original can be found in *Patterns of Learning*, published by the CLPE, Webber Row, London, SE1 8QW, in 1990. The scale describes aspects of bilingual students' development in their second language (L2). Elementary teachers have found it helpful in understanding and documenting progress in second language development, whether or not it is English. The scale describes predictable stages of language acquisition in broad terms, but it is important to recognize that each individual's language acquisition process is unique.

The scale considers the social as well as the academic aspects of language learning. That is, students may develop functional coping skills in a second language at a faster rate than they develop the kind of thoughtful, vocabulary-rich language necessary for scholastic success. Obviously, prevailing school attitudes about immigrant students and the languages they speak will influence their confidence and, therefore, their progress in using both their first and second languages.

STAGES IN ENGLISH LANGUAGE LEARNING

Language 1

Language 2

Stage1: New to English	Stage 2: Becoming Familiar with English	Stage 3: Becoming Confident as a User of English	Stage 4: A Very Fluent User of English
Makes contact with another child in the class. Joins in activities with other children, but may not speak. Uses nonverbal gestures to indicate meaning—particularly needs, likes, and dislikes. Watches carefully what other children are doing and often imitates them. Listens carefully and often "echoes" words and phrases of other children and adults. Needs opportunities for listening to the sounds, rhythms, and tunes of English through songs, rhymes, stories, and conversations. If young may join in repeating refrain of a story. Beginning to put words together into holistic phrases (e.g., no come here, where find it, not eating that). May be involved in classroom learning activities in the first language with children who speak the same first language. May choose to use first language only in most contexts. May be willing to write in the first language if she or he can, and if invited to do so. May be reticent with unknown adults. May be very aware of negative attitudes by peer group to the first language. May choose to move into English through story and reading, rather than speaking.	Growing confidence in using the English she or he is acquiring. Growing ability to move between the languages, and to hold conversations in English with peer group. Simple holistic phrases may be combined or expanded to communicate new ideas. Beginning to sort out small details (e.g., "he" and "she" distinction) but more interested in communicating meaning than in "correctness." Increasing control of the English tense system in particular contexts, such as storytelling, reporting events and activities that she or he has been involved in, and from book language. Understands more English than she or he can use. Growing vocabulary for naming objects and events, and beginning to describe in more detail (e.g., color, size, quantity) and use simple adverbs. Increasingly confident in taking part in activities with other children through English. Beginning to write simple stories, often modeled on those she or he has heard read aloud. Beginning to write simple accounts of activities she or he has been involved in, but may need support from adults and other children in her or his first language. Continuing to rely on support of friends.	Shows great confidence in using English in most social situations. This confidence may mask the need for support in taking on other registers (e.g., in science investigation, in historical research). Growing command of the grammatical system of English—including complex verbal meanings (relationships of time, expressing tentativeness and subtle intention with *might, could,* etc.) and more complex sentence structure. Developing an understanding of literary devices such as metaphor and pun. Pronunciation may be very native-speaker-like, especially that of young children. Widening vocabulary from reading stories, poems, and information books and from being involved in math and sciences investigations, and other curriculum areas. May choose to explore complex ideas (e.g., in drama/role play) in the first language with children who share the same first language.	A very experienced user of English, and exceptionally fluent in many contexts. May continue to need support in understanding subtle nuances of metaphor, and in Anglo-centric cultural content in poems and literature. Confident in exchanges and collaboration with English-speaking peers. Writing confidently in English with a growing competence over different genres. Continuing and new development in English drawn from own reading and books read aloud. New developments often revealed in own writing. Will move with ease between English and the first language depending on the contexts, what she or he judges appropriate, and the encouragement of the school.

For further information about this scale and/or the Learning Record Assessment System™, call or write the Center for Language in Learning, 10610 Quail Canyon Rd., El Cajon, CA 92021. Fax: 619-443-4698 or email: clrecord@cll.org.

The purpose of the following scale is to provide school faculties and those who support them with an instrument for assessing progress in implementing an effective performance assessment system. School staffs can use it to measure their own progress toward meeting the goal of a fully implemented system of assessment based on actual student work.

By determining together where they are now and what is next to be done, staff can set priorities for professional development. By involving parents and paraprofessionals in the process, they ensure their collaboration in the effort to improve the way student achievement is measured, reported, and understood by all stakeholders.

SCHOOL/DISTRICT PERFORMANCE ASSESSMENT IMPLEMENTATION SCALE

1 Preimplementation	2 Questioning	3 Beginning	4 Evolving	5 Student Work-Based Assessment System
■ Students rely on teacher evaluation of their work and assessment of their progress.	■ Students may be asked to save their work for assembling at the end of the term.	■ Students collect their work, reflect on it, or analyze it at the end of the term.	■ Students look at their work at the beginning and end of the semester or year in order to reflect on their progress. They note evidence of developing academic strengths.	■ Students regularly engage in reviewing their work in progress as well as upon its completion, seeking evidence that they are applying course content, learning strategies, and skills.
■ Teachers evaluate student achievement on individual assignments using idiosyncratic criteria based on often tacit, perhaps unexamined, standards.	■ Teachers, parents, and others in the school community begin to recognize a mismatch between what is being taught and what is being assessed. They question the value of reliance on norm-referenced, single-answer measures and may seek alternatives that provide information about student growth.	■ Teachers, alone or in collaboration, voice a need to review student work over time. They may apply standards or criteria supplied by others to the evaluation of their students' work. They take their impressions of student growth into account in planning for instruction.	■ Teachers help students use given criteria for evaluating their work. They review student work regularly, as a part of their work week, to make their criteria for judgment explicit and to determine the effectiveness of their instruction.	■ Teachers discuss standards for assessment among professional colleagues as well as parents and students, to arrive at local interpretations with locally produced illustrations of how well standards are being met.
■ External measures of student achievement are used mainly for placement and accountability purposes, and school staffs may try to identify classroom remedies for low test scores.	■ Administrators and some of the faculty consider possible advantages of assessing multiple samples of student work. They may begin to investigate the criteria others beyond the school/region are using to assess student work.	■ Tools such as a direct writing assessment or a collection of reading and/or math samples are employed to measure and describe student learning across classes and grade levels at the school.	■ Schoolwide assessment may focus on only one or two aspects of learning (e.g., writing and/or reading), but it nevertheless encourages authentic and thoughtful performance (e.g., writing in drafts over time, interpreting text responsibly).	■ All stakeholders, including parents, analyze assessment data regularly to improve both teaching and learning. Analysis focuses on the quality of multiple samples of student work—writing to learn and writing to be read by a range of audiences, reading many kinds of literary and informational text, listening and speaking for many purposes.
■ Students, parents, and teachers consider norm-referenced, single-answer tests to be the best way to measure knowledge and skills (e.g., spelling, punctuation, reading comprehension, computation, subject matter content).			■ Teachers, students, and parents share information gained from the assessment of student progress, using the same measurement criteria.	■ Teachers' judgments about the levels of student performance are based on documented evidence that can be validated in and beyond the school for consistency and fairness.

The Learning Record
(Elementary)

Adapted with permission from the Primary Language Record (PLR), Developed and copyrighted by the Centre for Language in Primary Education, Webber Row Teacher's Centre, Webber Row, London SE1 8QW, in 1988 and distributed in the U.S. by Heinemann Educational Books, Inc. ISBN 0-435-08516-6

School	Teacher	School Year

Name	Grade Level _____	Birth Date _____
	Boy/Girl _____	

Languages understood	Languages read	Languages spoken	Languages written

Details of any aspect of hearing, vision, or coordination affecting the child's language/literacy. Give the source and date of this information.	Names of staff involved with child's development.

PART A To be completed during the first quarter

A1 Record of discussion between child's parent(s) and class teacher   (LR Handbook for teachers K-6, Part A1)

Signed Parent(s) _____   Teacher _____

Date _____

A2 Record of language/literacy conference with child   (LR Handbook for teachers K-6, Part A2)

Date _____

Published as a component of The Learning Record Assessment System™. For further information, call or write the Center for Language in Learning at 10610 Quail Canyon Road, El Cajon, CA 92021 (619) 443-6320.

PART B To be completed during the second and/or third quarter and to include information from all teachers currently teaching the child.

  B1 Talking and Listening   (LR Handbook for Teachers K-6, Part B1)

Please comment on the child's development and use of spoken language in different social and curriculum contexts, in English and/or other languages: evidence of talk for learning and thinking; range and variety of talk for particular purposes; experience and confidence in talking and listening with different people in different settings.

What experiences and teaching have helped/would help development in this area? Record outcomes of any discussions with other staff or parent(s).

 B2 Reading   (LR Handbook for Teachers K-6, Part B2)

Please comment in your own words on the child's progress and development as a reader in English and/or other languages: the stage at which the child is operating; the range, quantity and variety of reading in all areas of the curriculum; the child's pleasure and involvement in story and reading, alone or with others; the range of strategies used when reading and the child's ability to reflect critically on what is read.   **Refer to the appropriate reading scale.**

Published as a component of The Learning Record Assessment System™. For further information, call or write the Center for Language in Learning at 10610 Quail Canyon Road, El Cajon, CA 92021 (619) 443-6320.

(B2 continued)

What experiences and teaching have helped/would help development in this area? Record outcomes of any discussions with other staff or parent(s).

B3 Writing   (LR Handbook for Teachers K-6, Part B2)

Please comment on the child's progress and development as a writer in English and/or other languages: the degree of confidence and independence as a writer; the range, quantity and variety of writing in all areas of the curriculum; the child's pleasure and involvement in writing, both narrative and non-narrative, alone and in collaboration with others; the influence of reading on the child's writing; growing understanding of written language, its conventions and spelling.
Refer to the appropriate writing scale

What experiences and teaching have helped/would help development in this area? Record outcomes of any discussions with other staff or parent(s).

Signed: Classroom Teacher _____ Date _____

Other Staff Contributor(s) _____ Date _____

_____ Date _____

Published as a component of The Learning Record Assessment System™. For further information, call or write the Center for Language in Learning at 10610 Quail Canyon Road, El Cajon, CA 92021 (619) 443-6320.

Student's placement on the reading and writing scales at
the end of third quarter
Reading- _____ Writing- _____

PART C To be completed during the fourth quarter   (LR Handbook for Teachers K-6, Part C)

C1 Comments on the record by the child's parent(s)

C2 Record of language/literacy conference with child

C3 Information for receiving teacher
This section is to ensure that information for the receiving teacher is as up to date as possible. Please comment on changes and development in any aspect of the child's learning since Part B was completed.

What experiences and teaching have helped/would help development in this area? Record outcomes of any discussions with other staff or parent(s).

Signed: Parent(s) _____ Date _____

Classroom Teacher _____ Date _____

Other Staff Contributor(s) _____ Date _____

Published as a component of The Learning Record Assessment System™. For further information, call or write the Center for Language in Learning at 10610 Quail Canyon Road, El Cajon, CA 92021 (619) 443-6320.

Data Collection

Name:

**Talking & Listening:
observation notes**

The space below is for recording examples of the child's developing use of talk for learning and interacting with others in English and/or other language:

Include different kinds of talk (e.g., planning an event, solving a problem, expressing a point of view or feeling, reporting on the results of an investigation, telling a story…).

Note the child's experience and confidence in handling social dimensions of talk (e.g., initiating a discussion, listening to another contribution, qualifying former ideas, encouraging others…).

The matrix sets out some possible contexts for Observing talk and listening. It may also be useful For addressing reading and writing development as well. Observations made in space below can be plotted on the matrix to record the range of socia and curriculum contexts sampled.

(LR Handbook for Teachers K-6, Part B)

Grade Level:

LEARNING CONTEXTS	SOCIAL CONTEXTS				
	pair	small group	child with adult	small or large group with adult	
collaborative reading and writing activities					
play, dramatic play, drama & storying					
environmental studies & historical research					
math & science investigations					
design, construction, crafts & arts projects					

Attach additional pages as necessary

Dates	Observations and their contexts

Published as a component of The Learning Record Assessment System ™. For further information, call or write the Center for Language in Learning, at 10610 Quail Canyon Road, El Cajon, CA 92021 (619) 443-6320.

2 Reading and Writing: observation notes

(Reading and writing in English and/or other languages)

(LR Handbook for teachers K-6, Part B)

Date		**Reading** Record observations of the child's development as a reader across a range of contexts and kinds of reading.

Date		**Writing** Record observations of the child's development as a writer (including stories dictated by the child when appropriate) across a range of contexts and kinds of writing.

Published as a component of The Learning Record Assessment System ™. For further information, call or write the Center for Language in Learning, at 10610 Quail Canyon Road, El Cajon, CA 92021 (619) 443-6320.

3 Reading Samples (Reading in English and/or other languages)   (LR Handbook for teachers K-6, Part B)
To include reading aloud and reading silently

Dates			
Title or book/text (literary or information)			
Known/unknown text			
Sampling procedure used: informal assessment/ running record/ miscue analysis			
Overall impression of the child's reading: • confidence and degree of independence • involvement in the book/text • the way in which the child reads the text aloud			
Strategies used when reading aloud: • drawing on previous experience to make sense of the book/text ____ * playing at reading * using book language * reading the pictures * focusing on print (directionality, 1:1 correspondence, recognition of certain words) ____ • using semantic, syntactic and graphophonic cues • predicting • self-correcting • using several strategies or over-dependence on one			
Child's response to the book/text: • personal response • critical response (understanding, evaluating, appreciating wider meanings			
What this sample shows about the child's development as a reader. **Experiences/support needed to further development.**			

* Early indicators that the child is moving into reading   Please attach text samples described on this sheet.

Published as a component of The Learning Record Assessment System ™. For further information, call or write the Center for Language in Learning, at 10610 Quail Canyon Road, El Cajon, CA 92021 (619) 443-6320.

4 Writing Samples (Writing in English and/or other languages)
Writing to include children's earliest attempts at writing

Dates			
Contexts and back-ground information about the writing • how the writing arose • how the child went about the writing • whether the child was writing alone or with others • whether the writing was discussed with anyone while the child was working on it • the kind of writing (e.g., list, letter, story, poem, personal writing, information writing) • complete piece of work/extract			
Child's own response to the writing.			
Teacher's response: • to the content of the writing • to the child's ability to handle this particular kind of writing • overall impressions			
Development of spelling and conventions of writing.			
What this writing shows about the child's development as a writer • how it fits into the range of the child's previous writing • experience/support needed to further development			

Please attach the writing with this sample sheet.

Published as a component of The Learning Record Assessment System ™. For further information, call or write the Center for Language in Learning, at 10610 Quail Canyon Road, El Cajon, CA 92021 (619) 443-6320.

References

Allen, B. M. 1998. *Deaf Children and the Families' Perspectives*. Unpublished dissertation, San Diego State University and Claremont Graduate University.

Arntson, D. 1994. *Reflective Reading: Self-Regulating Strategies for Emergent Readers*. Master's thesis, University of California at San Diego.

Barr, M. A. 1992. "The View from California." *Language Matters: English for Ages 5–16* (3): 28–29.

———. 1995a. "The California Learning Record System of Assessment Links Classroom and Board Room." *California Curriculum News Report 20* (March): 5.

———. 1995b. *California Learning Record: A Handbook for Teachers, Grades 6–12*. San Diego, CA: University of California at San Diego Bookstore.

———. 1995c. "Collecting Data, Telling Stories: Teacher Contributions to Classroom-Based Assessment." *Executive Summary of California Education 3* (2): 26–30.

———. 1995d. "Who's Going to Interpret Performance Standards? A Case for Teacher Judgment." In *Towards Multiple Perspectives on Literacy, Claremont Reading Conference 59th Yearbook*, ed. P. H. Dreyer, 22–45. Claremont, CA: Institute for Developmental Studies of The Claremont Graduate School.

———. 1997. "Linking Learning and Assessment." *Thrust for Educational Leadership* (February/March): 4–7.

Barr, M. A., and J. Cheong. 1995. "Achieving Equity: Counting on the Classroom." In *Equity and Excellence in Educational Testing and Assessment*, ed. M. T. Nettles and A. L. Nettles, 161–184. Boston: Kluwer Academic Publishers.

Barr, M. A., and P. J. Hallam. 1996. "Teacher Parity in Assessment with the California Learning Record." In *Writing Portfolios in the Classroom: Policy and Practice, Promise and Peril*, ed. R. A. Calfee and P. Perfumo, 285–302. Hillsdale, NJ: Lawrence Erlbaum Associates.

Barr, M. A., and M. A. Syverson. 1994. *California Learning Record: A Handbook for Teachers, K–6*. San Diego, CA: University of California at San Diego Bookstore.

Barrs, M., S. Ellis, H. Hester, and A. Thomas. 1988. *The Primary Language Record: Handbook for Teachers*. London: Centre for Language in Primary Education (CLPE) and Portsmouth, NH: Heinemann.

———. 1990. *Patterns of Learning: The Primary Language Record and the National Curriculum*. London: Centre for Language in Primary Education (CLPE).

Claggett, F. 1996. A *Measure of Success: From Assignment to Assessment in English Language Arts*. Portsmouth, NH: Boynton/Cook.

Clay, M. 1993. *An Observation Survey*. Portsmouth, NH: Heinemann.

Cooper, W., and M. Barr, eds. 1996. *The Primary Language Record and the California Learning Record in Use*. PLR/CLR International Seminar Proceedings: Center for Language in Learning, 10610 Quail Canyon Road, El Cajon, CA 92021.

Cowley, J. [1980], 1990. *The Hungry Giant*. Bothell, WA: Wright Group Shortland Publications.

Cushman, K. 1996. "The Primary Language Record & the California Learning Record." *Horace: A Publication of the Coalition of Essential Schools 13* (November): 5–6.

DeLawter, J., and C. Hendsch. 1992. "California Learning Record: Observations and Samples of Learning." In *Whole Language Catalog: Supplement on Authentic Assessment*, ed. K. S. Goodman, L. B. Bird, and Y. M. Goodman. Santa Rosa, CA: American School Publishers.

Fox, S. J. In press. "Student Assessment or What Is a Roach?" In *Next Steps: Research and Practice to Advance Indian Education*, ed. Swisher and J. Tippeconnic. ERIC, CRESS.

Ghio, J. 1998. "Becoming Accomplished as Readers in the High School Classroom with the Help of the Learning Record." *California English* (Summer): 11–13.

Goodman, Y., D. Watson, and C. Burke. 1987. *Reading Miscue Inventory: Alternative Procedures*. Katonah, NY: Richard C. Owen Publishers, Inc.

———. 1996. *Reading Strategies: Focus on Comprehension*. Katonah, NY: Richard C. Owen Publishers, Inc.

IRA/NCTE. 1995. *Standards for the Assessment of Reading and Writing*. International Reading Association/National Council of Teachers of English, Joint Task Force on Assessment.

Krimsly, S. and M. A. Barr. 1996. Learning Record web site (http://www.learningrecord.org/lrorg). Internet: Center for Language in Learning.

Martin, Jr., B. [1967], 1983. *Brown Bear, Brown Bear What Do You See?* New York City: Holt, Rinehart & Winston.

Miserlis, S. 1993. "The Classroom as an Anthropological Dig: Using the California Learning Record (CLR) as a Framework for Assessment and Instruction" In *The Claremont Reading Conference 57th Yearbook*, ed. Claremont, CA: Center for Developmental Studies of The Claremont Graduate School.

NCREST. 1993. "The California Learning Record." In *Authentic Assessment in Practice: A Collection of Portfolios, Performance Tasks, Exhibitions, and Documentation*, compiled by L. Darling-Hammond, L. Einbender, F. Frelow, and J. Ley-King, 279–306. New York City: National Center for Restructuring Education, Schools, and Teaching: Teachers College, Columbia University.

Neill, M. 1995. "Using Language Records (PLR/CLR) as Large-scale Assessments. *FairTest Examiner* (Summer), 8–9.

Neill, M., P. Bursh, B. Schaeffer, C. Thall, M. Yohe, and P. Zappardino. 1995. *Implementing Performance Assessments: A Guide to Classroom, School and System Reform*. Cambridge: FairTest: The National Center for Fair and Open Testing.

Rockwell, T. 1973. *How to Eat Fried Worms*. New York City: Bantam Doubleday Dell.

Syverson, M. A. 1996. Online Learning Record web site (http//www.cwrl.utexas.edu/~syverson/olr). Austin: University of Texas.

———. In Press. *The Wealth of Reality: An Ecology of Composition*. Southern Illinois University Press.

Thomas, S. 1993. "Rethinking Assessment: Teachers and Students Helping Each Other Through the 'Sharp Curves of Life.'" In *Learning Disability Quarterly 16* (Fall): 257–279.

Thomas, S. O. 1994. *Knowing Learners—Knowing Ourselves: Teachers' Perceptions of Change in Theory and Practice Resulting from Inquiry into Authentic Assessment*. Unpublished dissertation, Claremont Graduate School.